This book belongs to:

_____

# M *Is for* Mama

## Abbie Halberstadt
### Illustrations by Lindsay Long

**HARVEST HOUSE PUBLISHERS**
EUGENE. OREGON

Cover design by Faceout Studio
Cover photo © Artnis, Alexander Lysenko, natrot / Shutterstock
Interior design by Janelle Coury
Illustrations by Lindsay Long
Photo on page 4 by Jessica Helgesen Photography

For bulk, special sales, or ministry purchases, please call 1 (800) 547-8979.
Email: Customerservice@hhpbooks.com

# M Is for Mama

Copyright © 2022 by Abbie Halberstadt
Published by Harvest House Publishers
Eugene, Oregon 97408
www.harvesthousepublishers.com

ISBN 978-0-7369-8377-8 (hardcover)
ISBN 978-0-7369-8378-5 (eBook)

Library of Congress Control Number: 2021943911

**Printed in the United States of America**

23  24  25  26  27  28  29  30  / VP /  14  13  12  11  10  9  8

*For Alby.*
*Because you always believed I could.*
*You are my favorite. Really, really.*

# The Halberstadt Family

Shaun and Abbie

| | |
|---|---|
| Ezra (16) | Theo (7) |
| Simon (14) | Honor (5) |
| Della (11) | Shiloh (3) |
| Evy and Nola (9) | Titus and Tobias (1) |

# Contents

# Introduction

If you've got two X chromosomes, you can be a mother. The standards are so low-key that fully 50 percent of the world's population aces the qualification test before they've even taken one breath outside their own mothers' bellies.

But the physical ability to bear children does little to lessen the pang of panicked inadequacy almost every new mother feels upon being handed a tiny mewling infant to take home mere hours after forceful eviction from her body. We buckle their fragile, twiglike arms into a contraption made of plastic and foam and wonder if it should even be legal to grant someone with so little experience the primary task of raising another person from birth to adulthood.

I mean, think about it. People go to school for years to clean teeth. And yet it's okay to be given full responsibility for an actual human being with literally zero required reading, certifications, degrees, or crash courses of any kind.

And therein lies the mystery of motherhood.

We're expected to simply "get it." To "go with our guts." To be a natural baby whisperer. That all-encompassing rush of intense mother love we experience when we first lock eyes with our newborn covers a multitude of sins, right?

Well, yes. And no.

Because no matter how attached (or not) we feel to our babies, the fact of the matter is that instincts do little to combat silent reflux or calm a baby who refuses to latch *or* take a bottle. Or how about convincing the sweet little gal who thinks it's hilarious to wake up at 3:00 a.m. to pat your face and play that sleep is a better idea?

And then there's the fact that they're only babies for approximately 17 blinks of the eye before, suddenly, they're walking and talking and expressing opinions like "Ew" and "No" and "Sto-op!"

And yet again, the game has changed. And you're faced with an entirely new set of challenges and joys.

As a mama to many, with children in every age category from baby to teenager, I can assure you that the game never stops changing. At least, not in its particulars. There will always be some new wrinkle to iron out—that *one child* who breaks the mold entirely.

However, I firmly believe that the Bible has given us clear principles to live by that can make this whole motherhood gig a lot less intimidating and isolating. If Eve and Ruth and Rachel and Elizabeth and Mary and millions more in between were able to muddle through this mess of motherhood by God's grace, then so can we.

But we must be willing to heed the words of Proverbs 4:6-7: "Do not forsake wisdom, and she will protect you; love her, and she will watch over you. The beginning of wisdom is this: Get wisdom. Though it cost all you have, get understanding." Hosea 4:6 (esv) states it even more dramatically when it says, "My people are destroyed for lack of knowledge." The world may not officially require a degree for motherhood, but when we approach it with the same air of studiousness that we would any other profession at which we want to excel, we exponentially increase the likelihood of our not only surviving but thriving in a household of peace instead of chaos.

So where do we get this wisdom worth every penny we've got? Job 12:12 says, "Is not wisdom found among the aged? Does not long life bring understanding?" My favorite source of mama know-how is those godly women who have gone before me and "crash tested" so many different scenarios with their own kids. My own mother, who raised my brother and me. A precious friend and mama of twelve, almost twenty years my senior. Another wise mama of three who is a few years older than I. Sally Clarkson. Elisabeth Elliot. Ruth Bell Graham.

All these women have different numbers of children, mothering philosophies, personalities, and preferences. But they also have at least one thing in common that I want to emulate—something every godly mother should: a desire to "conduct [themselves] in a manner worthy of the gospel…without being frightened in any way by those who oppose [them]" (Philippians 1:27-28). That last bit is just as key as the first because, in a culture in which women clink their wine glasses in celebration each night for "surviving my kids for one more day," there will be many who oppose a view of motherhood that says that we can do more by Christ's strength.

Not only that, but there will be many who resent a perspective of motherhood that chooses to grasp hold of something other than the hard and the loss of "me time": namely, the abundant gems of joy and fulfillment that glitter amidst the everyday landscape of lunch prep, potty training, and sassy attitudes. Sometimes we just need someone to remind us of what an incredibly rad undertaking this whole motherhood gig really is.

Which is where I come in. I'm not even forty yet, so I don't qualify as "aged," but I am a mama of ten children. And I'm volunteering to be your cheerleader, your boot camp coach, your friend, and your fellow journeyer—"all things to all mamas," to paraphrase Paul. Because, while I do not have this whole mothering thing figured out or nailed down by any stretch, I have had enough practice applying some of the wise biblical principles I've learned from the women I listed above (and others) to get a pretty good feel for some strategies that are helpful to all mamas. For it is "a truth universally acknowledged: that a child in possession of a sinful nature must be in want of a mama who loves and seeks the Lord." (Sorry, Jane Austen. I had to.)

# The Culture of Mediocre Motherhood

## EXAMINING THE ATTITUDES THAT KEEP US FROM CHRISTLIKE EXCELLENCE

I have a feeling that the phrase "mediocre motherhood" will have quite the polarizing effect on the casual bookstore browser who happens to catch sight of this cover. A certain percentage of the population will immediately relate to it, assuming they know exactly what I mean. They may or may not be right. Another group might pick up this book and thumb through it out of sheer curiosity. What could this crazy lady with all these kids possibly mean by referring to motherhood of any kind as "mediocre"? And the last type of reader will probably pick up this book with the express intention of using it for kindling without ever cracking its spine. How *dare* I imply that any mother might possibly be less than a sparkly unicorn goddess warrior? After all, we have *given birth* or *gone through fire to choose our children.*

We are mothers. Hear us *roar*!

I'm sure I've missed a reaction or two, including that of utter indifference, but these are the three most prevalent possibilities that pop to mind, and so I feel compelled to explain, as clearly as I can, what I mean by such a loaded phrase.

But first, let's see what Merriam-Webster has to say about the word "mediocre." It describes someone or something as "of moderate or low quality, value, ability, or performance: ordinary, so-so."

Ouch, right?

It's not a state to which any human wants to aspire. Or at least, none *should* want to. And yet it's a state I can all too easily slide toward—and one to which our current mothering culture seems to gravitate.

In the words of *The Princess Bride*'s inimitable Inigo Montoya, "Let me 'splain."

## Why Relatable Is Not Always Reliable

My blog requires that I spend time on social media, interacting primarily with other mothers. And as anyone who has spent two minutes on Facebook or Instagram surely knows, social media is full of memes. Especially motherhood memes.

One in particular has stuck with me for years. It goes a little something like this:

> **God:** So how do you think you're doing as a mother?
>
> **Me:** Well, I fed my kids pizza almost every night this week, and I know I should read to them, but I don't really enjoy it, so I usually skip it. I've worn the same outfit three days in a row, and I can't remember the last time I washed my hair. I like our talks at dinner, but I worry a lot, so a lot of the time I'm thinking about stuff that's stressing me instead of really listening when my daughter tells me about her day, and I think she knows it. Most days, I'm too exhausted to do anything but watch Netflix all evening while I sip a couple of glasses of wine, and then I end up going to bed too late, so when I wake up in the morning to do it all over again, I'm really grouchy with my kids.
>
> **God:** But do you love them?

**Me:** With all my heart.

**God:** You sound like a wonderful mom to me.

Setting aside the contrived "conversation with God" construct of this meme, let's examine it a little more closely, shall we?

Here are the parts I don't give a rip about (you may feel differently). First, your three-day clothes. If you don't smell, and you haven't encountered the same people every single day (you know, besides your children and your husband), you can probably get away with this. Heaven knows I've thrown on the same top and jeans (and the same pj pants and tee) a couple of days in a row because they just ain't dirty enough to throw in the hamper. Also, about the unwashed hair thing, as a curly girl who washes her hair once a week *at most*, I am throwing zero shade in your direction over this. Unless it's grease city—in which case, girl, wash your hair.

Things start to get a little iffier for me with the pizza-on-repeat business. And not because I don't love a good pie every now and again. I'm also not a stickler for organic or hemp hearts or kombucha (though all three can be stellar life choices), but I do feel like we, as the providers of sustenance, should be making an effort here. Our children's health is a big deal, and a steady diet of pizza (or chicken nuggets or boxed mac and cheese) is only going to go so far toward giving them the good stuff their bodies and brains need to thrive.

From this point on, the meme completely falls apart for me. And it's *not* because I can't relate to not particularly enjoying certain activities with my kids, worrying too much and listening too little, or wanting to do nothing more than veg on the sofa every evening.

Because I can.

I think all those are perfectly normal escapist responses to the overwhelm that motherhood can bring. And they are the first doors that my tired self wants to walk through when I'm given the option to choose. But here's the thing: Just because something is relatable doesn't mean it's not mediocre.

*Just because something is relatable doesn't mean it's not mediocre.*

In fact, relatability can stray far past mediocrity and nose-dive into outright petty meanness. Another meme that I stumbled upon went a little something like this: "You're not a real mother unless you've given your three-year-old the finger behind your back today." Based on the hundreds of enthusiastically affirmative responses, I couldn't help but conclude that this was a highly relatable sentiment for this poster's audience (which was, presumably, comprised of women who had mothered at least one three-year-old).

The thing is, I've parented eight three-year-olds so far, and while "giving the finger" isn't really on my radar, I can't deny the ungodly anger that has welled up in my soul at times over the actions of a tiny human who only recently stopped wearing a diaper.

It's ridiculous (I mean, we're the adults in this scenario), but it's also relatable. Which is why I feel I must reiterate: Relatability—while helpful at times—is not the gold standard of motherhood.

And that very relatability is, all too often, the rotten core of the argument that says, "If this many mothers also feel this way, it must be right and true."

Thank God that we have his Holy Word, the Bible, to combat this kind of reasoning. Paul, the "super apostle" himself, says, "For I know that nothing good dwells in me, that is, in my flesh. For I have the desire to do what is right, but not the ability to carry it out. For I do not do the good I want, but the evil I do not want is what I keep on doing" (Romans 7:18-19 ESV).

Talk about the height of relatability (how many times have I mentally bemoaned my inability to resist that cinnamon roll or bowl of ice cream I *know* I don't really need?)—except with a solid undergirding of truth. The first meme I mentioned expresses a kind of wistfulness—almost a wishing that the mother in the scenario *could* do better—then ends with a shrug of acknowledgment (and an A-okay from God) that "it is what it is." And the

It's not our bad days
or our hormones
that are the real hang-ups
but instead
our inability to be anything
other than mediocre
without Christ.

second meme is full of angry defiance. Yes, my attitude toward my own child is one of rage and impatience, but so what? Everybody feels this way.

Neither acknowledges that the real root of the issue is our own sinful mothering tendencies. Because it's not our bad days or our hormones or our understandably tired responses that are the real hang-ups here. The true culprit? Our inability to be anything other than mediocre without Christ.

Sure, we can bootstrap our way through a day, a week, a month, or even a year. But without Christ's transforming power at work in us, we will inevitably slide back into our patterns of complacency or anger. For as Philippians 2:13 (ESV) says, "It is God who works in you, both to will and to work for his good pleasure." The most disciplined of us might be able to maintain a veneer of schedules and control most of the time, but true excellence—the kind that comes from a renewed mind and heart—can only flow from the Holy Spirit's pricking of our consciences and what Ephesians 5:26 describes as "the washing with water through the word."

I experienced just such a conscience pricking when I was in the throes of first-trimester exhaustion and nausea during my pregnancy with Honor. We had a family wedding looming, and I was hoping to find just the right dress to accommodate my awkward "is-she-or-isn't-she" bump. I didn't care nearly as much about the dress as my hours spent scrolling the internet implied. It was the mindless distraction from my pregnancy misery that I craved. I knew I should read my Bible with at least as much fervor as I cross-referenced dress sales and that I should go to bed at a decent time so that I had the energy both my growing baby and my other children required. But I stubbornly clung to my right to "check out" each evening after the kids had gone to bed. Even as I defensively told myself that this was "my time" and that my nightly mental escape wasn't affecting anyone else, the Lord was gently poking and prodding at my stubborn heart. He reminded me that even though wedding-party dress shopping isn't mediocre, devoting myself to it to the detriment of my family or my relationship with him is.

I'm fairly certain most pregnant moms have shared my hormone-fueled feelings of escapism, at least briefly. So what am I proposing? If relatability

IT IS God WHO WORKS IN YOU.

PHILIPPIANS 2:13

is mediocrity (it isn't always, by the way), then what exactly are we called to be as mothers? Is this some sort of competition to collect accolades from our peers? Are we called to be a generation of Tiger Moms with perfectly coiffed hair (nope), polished children (nuh-uh), and Instagram-worthy quiet times with the Lord (ha!)?

Can you tell yet that my answer is a thousand times no?

## A Sacred Sameness

In fact, rather than making this about being better or different from any other mom out there, I'm proposing that we pursue conformity. But not conformity to our cultural norm. If that's what we're chasing, we may discover that we fit in just fine and can always manage to find someone to justify our shortcomings or make us feel better about our bad days. But we will not have found, at the end of it all, that we look much like Jesus or that we have gotten any closer to feeling at peace with motherhood. The only way to effect real change—the kind that produces lasting joy and fulfillment—is to pursue what Romans 8:29 calls conformity to the image of Christ.

We are *all* supposed to be like Christ—a kind of sacred sameness that unites rather than divides us. The basics of Christlike conformity are identical for all of us: repentance, salvation, Scripture, prayer, loving the Lord our God, and loving our neighbor as ourselves. But the particular ways in which we express our devotion to him will be different for each individual mama, depending on temperament, background, personality, resources, and giftings.

In this digital age, we have access to what *seems* like a front-row seat to other people's entire lives—their children, their vacations, the books they read, the clothes they wear. It's tempting to study what others do and err on one side or the other of the comparison spectrum. Either we will feel superior when we notice someone struggling in an area in which we excel, or we will begin to doubt our own giftings when we see someone who seems to be doing particularly well. "I'm not artsy or creative," we'll think. "So I can't possibly be a super-engaging mom like Willow. Look at all the amazing hands-on projects she does with her children." Or "I'm not organized like Suzy. Surely my kids would be better off if I had more labeled bins in my pantry."

Of course, the truth is that while we are *all* created in God's image, he has graciously granted us different aspects of his nature, and that is where the sameness ends. And praise the Lord for that! The world would be a chaotic place with all art projects and no organization. Likewise, it would be a very dull place indeed with only label makers and no creative free play.

Excellent motherhood in Christ is achievable through a myriad of biblically sound paths. That is freeing news! We do not have to be slaves to the culture of mediocre motherhood, which says, "I stank at motherhood today. You too?" We do not have to find solace in the knowledge that wine o'clock is coming (I am not objecting to wine specifically but rather the dependence on it). We do not have to find our identity in fist bumps of solidarity with similarly burned-out moms. Fist bumps are awesome and burnout is real. And there is nothing wrong with acknowledging the hard and seeking encouragement.

> *We do not have to be slaves to the culture*
> *of mediocre motherhood, which says,*
> *"I stank at motherhood today. You too?"*

But when our goal is validation rather than Christ, it ultimately pushes us down into the mire of self-focus and, all too often, self-pity. Jesus holds out his hand to draw us up to excellent motherhood in freedom, giving us the ability to pursue it through the unique strengths (and weaknesses) he has blessed us with. Biblical motherhood encourages us to look outside ourselves—at our children, our homes, our husbands, our friends, and our communities at large—and find ways to overcome mediocrity and uplift each other in the spirit of a mutual (and yet gloriously varied) pursuit of righteousness.

Note: As a busy mama, I know there are many times I have read and even agreed with a chapter in a book, only to immediately dive into another task without fully processing what I have just ingested. I wanted to give you something to help your brain continue to chew on what you have read as you go about your daily responsibilities. So at the end of each chapter, I've provided a few takeaways (called "The Narrative"), some action steps, questions for personal reflection, and a prayer. I pray these tools will help you absorb the information and apply it to your life!

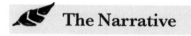 **The Narrative**

| MEDIOCRE MOTHERHOOD | CHRISTLIKE MOTHERHOOD |
|---|---|
| Wallows in struggles, resulting in prolonged anger or apathy | Acknowledges struggles but leans on the Lord for strength and direction |
| Sees community as a source of self-affirmation | Sees community as a source of encouragement and wisdom |
| Seeks approval for mediocrity | Seeks to "do better" through Christ |

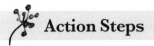

## Action Steps

- Memorize and meditate on Proverbs 11:14 (ESV): "Where there is no guidance, a people falls, but in an abundance of counselors there is safety."
- Make a list of three Christlike mamas whom you could seek out for help and guidance.
- Unfollow accounts that glorify and glamorize snark, hopelessness, or abdication of responsibility in motherhood.

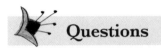

## Questions

Am I using Scripture as my standard for excellence in motherhood?

Do I feel validated when I see others struggling (and failing) in the same areas as I am?

Am I willing to make changes to my attitudes and behavior when the Holy Spirit convicts me?

## Prayer

*Lord, thank you for giving wisdom generously and without reproach to all who ask (James 1:5). May we turn to you each day in every area of our lives, including motherhood, recognizing that conformity to Christ is infinitely better than fitting in with the world.*

# No Two Good Mamas Look Alike

## KICKING COMPARISON AND EMBRACING OUR GIFTINGS IN CHRIST

I host a workout group at my home for a troop of mamas who have become some of my dearest friends and most kindred spirits. I've been a fitness instructor for fifteen years, but this group came about seemingly serendipitously (although I can clearly see God's handiwork in it now). Several years ago, while on a girls' trip to Joanna Land (a.k.a. Magnolia) with some new friends from a church we had recently started attending, I listened as several expressed a desire for regular workout accountability. Gym membership fees were prohibitive for some, lack of childcare for others, and personal motivation for all. Suddenly, a thought popped into my mind, and before I could examine it too closely, I blurted out, "If I offered my home for classes, would any of you be interested in coming?" And almost all of them immediately blurted back, "Yes!"

## A Sisterhood of Encouragement

And thus began our home workout group—attended by up to ten ladies (and *all* their offspring), but with a rock-solid core group of five. It has been one of the biggest blessings of my life in recent years. We have all grown to know and love each other more as we sweat, eat lunches, plan playdates, and chase babies. *Together.* All these women represent my fervent prayers with skin on them—the incarnate answers to years of beseeching God for genuine community. (I really do mean *years,* friends. If you're still praying for this kind of sisterhood, don't give up.)

But do you know what I love most about this group? No two of us are alike. Two are moms of three whose kids attend public school. Two of us, a mama of four and I, homeschool. One has children who attend a private school, even though her husband is a public school principal. Some of us vaccinate; some do not. Some of us slather our children in crunchy-granola hippie goop (a.k.a. essential oils), and others think that's quackery. But we have *never once* had an argument about the "best" way to school our children or treat their illnesses or correct an attitude. I kid you not. We have shared strategies, prayed over each other, and learned from one another, but we have never clashed, because we know that each of us loves our children unequivocally and desires God's best for them. We also recognize that each of us has specific strengths and weaknesses that uniquely gift us to excel in certain areas while limiting our abilities in others. It's such a beautiful example of Hebrews 10:24-25 (ESV), which says, "And let us consider how to stir up one another to love and good works, not neglecting to meet together, as is the habit of some, but encouraging one another, and all the more as you see the Day drawing near."

This spirit of camaraderie and encouragement is rare, even among genuine Christians. As someone who prayed all the more intensely for this kind of support group because of comparison and competition-filled relationships in my past, I can personally attest to the joy and freedom that comes with watching others walk in their own unique callings as mothers.

And because we have each other's best interests at heart, we don't hesitate to give a shout-out to one another for the things we do well. I remember receiving a text from one member of the group that came at the perfect time. I was twenty-three weeks pregnant with Titus and Tobias at the time and feeling tired and hormonal. We had had an unusually busy week of errands and appointments, and the laundry was piling up while my toilets got grungier by the day. Nothing drove this reality deeper into my brain than the sparkling floors and pristine baseboards of a friend's house we visited that week. Even though I knew she had outside cleaning help (and I did not) and even though she's a dear friend whom I admire greatly, I was letting my hormonal emotions drag me into the pit of comparison. "What's wrong with you, Halberstadt?" (Not sure why I sometimes mentally refer to myself by my last name like a crotchety high school football coach.) "Why can't you get your act together and have everything as constantly spick-and-span as she does?"

There were some obvious answers beyond the cleaning lady. She wasn't pregnant with twins. She has fewer kids and a smaller house. She was aware that people were coming over to her house, so comparing her "company-ready" status to my "middle-of-the-day mess" was unfair. And she has a meticulous, orderly, clean-loving personality (while also having an incredible heart for hospitality). I enjoy having a clean home and strive for neatness and order, but it is not something that comes completely naturally to me. I have to work at it; she can't function without it.

In short, she and I are different people. There are many things I can learn from her example, but I cannot exchange personalities with her, nor should I want to, since that is an affront to the ways in which God has uniquely crafted me.

But back to that timely text I mentioned. After one of our exercise sessions at my house, a regular attendee sent me this message: "Just in case I haven't said it recently, being in your home is always so refreshing. I really do sigh as I drive in your driveway. Thank you for being so hospitable."

What a kind thing to say, right? And what an affirmation of the hospitality that I *knew* the Lord wanted us to offer when we spent two years building this house with our own hands while raising a passel of babies. I immediately felt my silly stresses about not measuring up to my friend's gleaming house standards fall away. The Lord can still use my home to bless others, even if the shower grout needs scrubbing and there are dishes in the sink.

# Walking Through the Narrow Gate
## of Our God-Given Calling

Conversely, I can't tell you how many times I've received a message through one of my blog channels expressing despair at ever measuring up to *my* standards. "I'm so overwhelmed with two kids, and you make it look so easy with five times that many," they'll say. Or "I don't know *how* you find time to exercise on top of everything else."

Here's the thing: I'm one of those weirdos who love to exercise. It is life-giving to me. It also helps me have more energy and a better attitude toward my family. I'm willing to wake up early to do it (I teach morning fitness classes before 6:00 a.m.) or endure inconvenience to make it happen (I have done many a kickboxing session at my home while ducking and weaving around three or four small humans like a considerably less cool Bruce Lee in one of his famous "group fight" scenes). But it doesn't mean that other things don't feel like too much to me. So this is what I tell these precious, freaked out, discouraged mamas: "Everything you see me doing well is either the result of a natural personality bent or years of the Lord's molding my weaknesses into something that more closely resembles the way I was uniquely designed to reflect his image."

He's not done with me yet, and I know he's not done with you either. Seek him. Ask his guidance about where your time is best spent. Follow through when he provides direction, even if it's not your favorite. Even when it's hard. Because hard is not the same thing as bad. (You'll read this phrase more than once in this book.) You will see growth. You will see progress. He will sustain you through it. Never compare your beginning or middle to anyone else's *anything*. There is no such thing as a one-size-fits-all good mama.

*Never compare your beginning or middle to anyone else's anything. There is no such thing as a one-size-fits-all good mama.*

Maybe the Lord has given you a passion for coupon clipping (which makes my brain hurt), running a hobby farm (So. Much. Work.), or mentoring younger women (now *this* I love!). Maybe writing a blog sounds utterly overwhelming but baking bread to deliver to neighbors doesn't. Maybe volunteering isn't feasible but being a prayer warrior is.

> For just as the body is one and has many members, and all the members of the body, though many, are one body, so it is with Christ. For in one Spirit we were all baptized into one body—Jews or Greeks, slaves or free—and all were made to drink of one Spirit. For the body does not consist of one member but of many. If the foot should say, "Because I am not a hand, I do not belong to the body," that would not make it any less a part of the body. And if the ear should say, "Because I am not an eye, I do not belong to the body," that would not make it any less a part of the body. If the whole body were an eye, where would be the sense of hearing? If the whole body were an ear, where would be the sense of smell? But as it is, God arranged the members in the body, each one of them, as he chose. If all were a single member, where would the body be? As it is, there are many parts, yet one body (1 Corinthians 12:12-20 ESV).

"Drinking of one Spirit" may sound kind of mystical, but really all it means is that as Christians, we all get our marching orders, varied as they are in their particulars, from the same source. If you are a believer, the only other "people" who truly need to approve of your mothering are God, Jesus, and the Holy Spirit. So when we are tempted to self-flagellate because we can't find time to make kombucha or homemade sourdough like our neighbor, may we instead remind ourselves that "whether [we] eat or drink or whatever [we] do, do it all for the glory of God" (1 Corinthians 10:31).

Jill Churchill, a mystery novelist, famously said, "There's no way to be a perfect mother and a million ways to be a good one." It's no mystery (ha, see what I did there?) she is one smart cookie. Of course, we have only to overhear a mom gripe session in the grocery store, observe a toxic, jealousy-fueled relationship between two mamas, or as I talked about in the last

WHETHER YOU **EAT** OR **DRINK** OR WHATEVER YOU DO, DO IT ALL FOR THE **GLORY** OF **GOD**.

1 CORINTHIANS 10:31

chapter, take a peek at popular social media accounts to discover just how many ways there are to be a mediocre mama too.

Being bad at fitting in a daily workout does not make you a mediocre mama. Being a less than creative home chef does not make you a mediocre mama. Being a late riser does not make you a mediocre mama.

But shirking? Complaining? Participating in the "mommy wars" of shaming and one-upping? Ignoring our God-given callings?

All of these are at least warning signals that we are succumbing to the pressure to conform to the world's mediocre standards rather than God's excellent ones. This path may provide brief flashes of justification—"At least I'm not doing *that*," or "See, she struggles with the same thing"—but it will never fill us with a lasting assurance that we are walking in the narrow way, the only one that promises *life*.

For it was Jesus himself who commanded us to "enter through the narrow gate. For wide is the gate and broad is the road that leads to destruction, and many enter through it. But small is the gate and narrow the road that leads to life, and only a few find it" (Matthew 7:13-14).

I know this is a verse about salvation, but I don't think that I'm taking it *too* far out of context to also apply it to the ways in which we continue in that salvation on a path of righteousness.

You've probably figured out by now that I don't think every single "narrow gate" of motherhood will have the same initials stamped on it. In fact, if it doesn't have your name on it, I highly encourage you to keep on walking without even looking at what's going on in that particular pasture. But when you find your gate, you must walk through it and stay the course. Motherhood is so much more than feel-good affirmations that there is no wrong way to mother (spoiler alert: There is). That platitude has been the undoing of too many well-meaning, tired moms for me to treat it as anything other than the dangerous untruth it is.

*Motherhood is so much more than feel-good affirmations that there is no wrong way to mother (spoiler alert: There is).*

In fact, James 4:17 (ESV) says, "So whoever knows the right thing to do and fails to do it, for him it is sin." Like, whoa. Am I saying that *inaction* can be sin? Yep. When the Lord leads us to our very own narrow gate emblazoned with our name in bold sans serif font, if we peer beyond, notice some craters in the road, and think, "Nah, I'm good, Lord. Thanks, but I'll stay right here in my comfortable place," we are literally committing sin.

In other words, when I said that being bad at fitting in workouts doesn't make you a mediocre mom, it was true—*unless* you have a conviction from the Lord that your health needs to be more of a priority. The same is true of meals, bedtimes and rising times, how we dress, who we spend time with, and the list goes on. If the Holy Spirit is whispering "Do better" in our ears, it doesn't really matter how many times or in how many ways we shove him away. It doesn't matter who else *isn't* getting the same memo. We will never have peace until we address those areas of growth. And anything resembling peace that we do achieve while tuning out the gentle nudging of God's Spirit will be a false sense of comfort balanced precariously on a foundation of sin.

I know, I know. I kind of dropped the hammer there. But while it may feel like I've shifted gears from "I'm okay, you're okay" to "Sin, *sin,* SIN!" the reality is that a recognition of our giftings and a willingness to actually walk in them are two very different things. Because the ultimate issue is not whether God can use us in unique ways to bless our families (he can) but whether we are too focused on what others are doing or too focused on making excuses about our insecurities to follow through on his leading.

Yes, there are a million different ways to be a good mom. But in which areas has the Lord given us special gifts, and are we actually receiving them? Neither the world nor our friends nor our mom can answer this question for

If the Holy Spirit is whispering "Do better" in our ears, it doesn't matter who else isn't getting the same memo.

us. Only we can. Saying yes to God's leading takes a great deal more courage than choosing either defeat or a sense of false superiority. And answering his calling, rather than trying to measure up to our peers, is the only guaranteed way of being the best mamas we possibly can be.

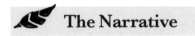 **The Narrative**

| MEDIOCRE MOTHERHOOD | CHRISTLIKE MOTHERHOOD |
|---|---|
| Gets bogged down in the details of what others are doing | Makes the most of the talents we've been given |
| Makes excuses based on others' "performances" | Takes responsibility for improving on weaknesses |
| Lives in fear of failure | Rests in Christ's "enoughness" |

 **Action Steps**

- Memorize and meditate on 2 Corinthians 10:12 (ESV): "Not that we dare to classify or compare ourselves with some of those who are commending themselves. But when they measure themselves by one another and compare themselves with one another, they are without understanding."

- Make a list of three things the Lord has given you the ability to do well and three things you struggle with.

- Choose one thing you can do this week to exercise a particular gifting and one thing you can do to strengthen an area in which you are weak.

 **Questions**

Am I avoiding community because I'm afraid I won't measure up?

Do I tend to look down on others who aren't "performing" as well as I am?

Am I using my giftings to bless my children and others?

 **Prayer**

*Lord, you say in your Word that those who compare and measure themselves by others for their worth are not wise (2 Corinthians 10:12). Please help us to be grateful for the things you've made us good at and willing to work on the areas in which we struggle.*

# What Is That to You?
# Follow Me

## STAYING THE COURSE REGARDLESS
## OF WHAT ANYONE ELSE IS DOING

I have a weekly bit I do on my Instagram account called "Whaddya Wanna Know Wednesday." I invite readers, "Ask me anything, and I'll answer as many questions as I can." I don't spend a significant portion of most days on social media (hello: ten kids), but I budget up to two hours (spread throughout the day) to answering questions each Wednesday.

I have been asked everything from what products I use on my hair and my best tips for potty training to my thoughts on different Christian denominations and how to have "the talk" with a child (more on that later). We cover a plethora of topics, and while I don't shy away from the hard questions, I sometimes find myself biting my virtual tongue when it comes to certain questions.

What kind of questions?

I'm glad you asked. The queries that give me the most pause are not of the knotty theological variety, or even those that flirt with "mommy wars" topics, but the ones worded in such a way that implies that the person asking is determined to follow to the letter whatever my answer happens to be.

Or, conversely, those that are worded with the obvious intent to "out me" for doing it wrong.

*To fashion our lives after anyone but Christ is a shaky enterprise indeed.*

Yo, that's a lot of pressure. To fashion our lives after anyone but Christ is a shaky enterprise indeed. And for anyone to use *me* as a litmus test for godliness is pure foolishness—not because I don't get some things right by the grace of God but because I, just like everyone else, am capable of failing spectacularly. And if anyone's hope is in *my* goodness, it will be disappointed. Guaranteed.

Paul said it best: "For when one of you says, 'I follow Paul,' and another, 'I follow Apollos'…what then is Apollos? And what is Paul? They are servants through whom you believed, as the Lord has assigned to each his role" (1 Corinthians 3:4-5 bsb).

## Only Christ Is Worth Emulating

And so I strive to remind my readers (and myself) daily that as Jesus said in Mark 10:18, "No one is good—except God alone." (Of course, Jesus said this knowing that he himself *is* God, a subtle declaration of his deity.) Not only that, but God has revealed his goodness to us in the pages of Scripture. So even though it can be super helpful to pick the brain of a mama who has "gone before" you on the path of motherhood (one of the reasons I wrote this book!), and Titus 2 gives a great outline for womanly mentorship, it's crucial to ground in Christ alone any sense of identity that we hold. When we are secure in that identity, we can take anything anyone else says or does with a spiritual grain of salt—especially if that advice is grounded in anything other than Bible truth.

*When we are secure in that identity, we can take anything anyone else says or does with a spiritual grain of salt—especially if that advice is grounded in anything other than Bible truth.*

That's not to say that we can't glean truth from nonbelievers. Brené Brown and I differ greatly in our opinions about many things, and yet she spoke to this very issue when she said, "You either walk into your story and own your truth, or you live outside of your story, hustling for your worthiness."[1] Of course, this "bootstrap" mentality completely excludes the sovereignty of God, and yet the truth of it still rings. If we rely on others to reveal our purpose to us, rather than owning the truth of who God says we are in him (forgiven: 1 John 1:9; beloved: Colossians 3:12; precious: Isaiah 43:4; unique: Psalm 139:14), we will continually be chasing external approval, or even permission, to walk in the paths God has clearly laid out for us.

As I've already mentioned, the opposite response is also true. All too often, paying too much attention to what someone else is doing can cause us to feel threatened if it doesn't align with our own paradigm—even if it's something that shouldn't matter at all (remember my insecure response to my friend's pristine house?). I can't tell you how many times I've shared a recipe only to be asked, "Are you *sure* that's enough food for your whole family? I feel like my family of four eats more than that." The fact that another family's food consumption genuinely concerns anyone proves that when we fix our eyes on others rather than Christ, we are capable of resenting, or at least second-guessing, just about anything.

Another good example is family size. As a much-larger-than-usual family, we draw many comments and stares whenever we're all in public together. *Especially* with the dynamic of two sets of identical twins.

Many people are effusive in their encouragement.

"What a gorgeous family you have!"

"My goodness, you sure are blessed!"

"Look at all those sweet kids!"

But the opposite response is more common than I would like, particularly when it happens in front of my children. I have been told by a stranger that if she had "that many kids" (at the time, I had six with me), she would "kill herself." I have been chastised online for my carbon footprint. Some have speculated that I only get pregnant again for the publicity. (As someone who is *not* a fan of pregnancy, I find the thought of enduring nine difficult months, followed by at least eighteen years of responsibility for another human, just to get a few extra likes, to be nothing short of snort-worthy.)

Conversely, I've heard from many moms who feel shamed by MOMs (Mothers of Many) for "only" having one or two kids. They feel "less than" because of the dismissive comments or eye rolls. And the culprits are often fellow Christian mamas. When I hear this, I can't help but think of James 3:10 (BSB): "Out of the same mouth come blessing and cursing. My brothers [sisters!], this should not be!"

It makes my heart so heavy to hear these things.

## Staying in Our Christ-Given Lane

As Christians, we are admonished in 1 Thessalonians 5:21 (ESV) to "test everything" and to "hold fast to what is good." We don't just yawn at sin. We examine people's words and actions for biblical truth. But (and this is a biggie) in circumstances of *preference* or freedom in Christ, embarking on a holy crusade to convert everyone else to our way of thinking will never end the way we hope. Even if we do win over a few "disciples," unless our goal is to point them to their identity in Christ, the "conversion" will be a shallow one indeed.

*We don't just yawn at sin. We examine people's words and actions for biblical truth. But (and this is a biggie) in circumstances of preference or freedom in Christ, embarking on a holy crusade to convert everyone else to our way of thinking will never end the way we hope.*

It's almost as if God has placed us on this narrow highway called the Christian Life and then painted bold yellow double "do not cross" lines down the center to ensure that we don't wander from our lane into oncoming traffic. Ignoring those lines can all too often result in wrecked relationships and shattered hearts. It's simply not worth the collateral damage, especially when it takes our focus off God's path for *us*.

So does that mean we're never allowed to look at what others are doing? That doing so is inherently sinful? Of course not. There's quite a difference between noting the make and model of a passing car and veering across the line markers to smash into it. As I mentioned above, I am often asked what I do to relax and de-stress. How I prioritize "me time." When I exercise and how. What I eat. How I parent. What I watch. And I have asked fellow mamas many of the same questions.

Healthy curiosity is a part of the learning process called life. But a desire to know what else is out there and how to grow from it is different from a desire either to emulate (because we are unsure of who we are) or to excoriate (because we are offended by anyone who disagrees with us).

I want to be crystal clear about this issue because I will be sharing with you in upcoming chapters some of the practical things we do as a family to thrive in our Christ-given lane. I hope they are helpful to you, no matter your personality or family size. It is my goal to share only those things that

Opportunities for distraction, excuses, and envy abound, but the answer is always the same: Follow Jesus.

can be viewed as truth principles—I won't be telling you whether or not to cloth diaper or use certain medicines or buy organic vegetables—because anything more is getting dangerously close to my "double lines."

## But What Does the Bible Say About It?

Several years ago, on a day when my mom had come over to hold down the fort so I could work on writing this very chapter, I shared my frustrations with the specificity of some of my "Whaddya Wanna Know Wednesday" questions. Questions about how to make friends if your neighborhood consists of only people of a certain age. Or how to parent a twenty-month-old who has a specific behavioral quirk. Or what to do if a girlfriend makes a particular snarky remark about your child. My desire is to point women to Christ, not teach them to do things "Abbie style." So while I could answer each exact question down to its particular details, what I *try* to do is always redirect the question-asker to certain scriptural principles that never fail.

As I bemoaned the stickiness of giving the "right response," my mom, who is very wise but also very practical, said, "These women need to read their Bibles! Pretty much everything in life can be boiled down to a handful of fundamental scriptural truths."

I responded that value exists in getting sound advice on particular topics (and she agreed), but I couldn't help but think that if we all had a little more of my mom's mic-drop attitude toward the challenges and choices we face in life, we might spend less time wallowing around in the quagmires of indecision, comparison, and conflict. And we might make fewer excuses for our sin.

*Pretty much everything in life can be boiled down to a handful of fundamental scriptural truths.*

In friendships, we would be quick to extend a hand to all, no matter their age, without demanding that our needs be met in return.

In parenting, we would dig deep into training and consistency, no matter the age or the issue.

In confronting unkindness, we would respond with goodwill.

Of course, because of sin, none of us is capable of executing these things perfectly all the time. But when we know *whose* we are and what his Word has to say to us, the answers are surprisingly straightforward.

Be kind (Ephesians 4:32).

Don't complain or argue (Philippians 2:14).

Never gossip (1 Timothy 5:13).

Assume the best (1 Corinthians 13:7).

Don't be afraid of hard things (Joshua 1:9).

All these precepts and more can be found in the pages of Scripture and in the example of Christ's life, which is, after all, the only one worth emulating.

On the topic of overthinking what everyone around us is doing, Oswald Chambers said this:

> Your part is to maintain the right relationship with God so that His discernment can come through you continually for the purpose of blessing someone else.... Maturity is produced in the life of a child of God on the unconscious level, until we become so totally surrendered to God that we are not even aware of being used by Him.[2]

So the next time we find out that a friend is having another baby, and we feel either envious or judgmental, may we look instead to what Scripture says about babies (they are a blessing, regardless of the number—Psalm 127:3).

Or maybe we'll be tempted to join our friends who identify as Christians in watching that dating show full of extramarital sex and "follow your heart" mantras—because "it's fun." Instead, may we continue to trust that when Philippians 4:8 encourages us to dwell on "whatever is true, whatever is noble, whatever is right, whatever is pure," it's for our own good and for God's glory.

In other words, regardless of what any other mother out there—Christian or secular—is doing, our job is to stay in the lane the Lord has laid out for us through his Word and the prompting of his Holy Spirit. I can't help but think of the time that Peter, walking with Jesus after his resurrection, glanced back and noticed John following (John 21:21-22). "What about him?" he asked. (Sound familiar? Clearly, it's not just a thing we women do.)

And Jesus issued a mic drop of his own: "If I want him to remain alive until I return, what is that to you? You must follow me."

Opportunities for distraction, excuses, and envy abound, but the answer is always the same: Follow Jesus.

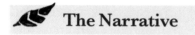 **The Narrative**

| MEDIOCRE MOTHERHOOD | CHRISTLIKE MOTHERHOOD |
| --- | --- |
| Trusts the status quo for "truth" | Looks to Scripture for truth |
| Feels insecure and defensive | Is confident in her identity in Christ |
| Is swayed by popular opinion | Holds fast to biblical conviction |

 **Action Steps**

- Memorize and meditate on Galatians 1:10 (ESV): "For am I now seeking the approval of man, or of God? Or am I trying to please man? If I were still trying to please man, I would not be a servant of Christ."

- Talk to your kids about what it looks like to follow Jesus even when no one else is. Take note of the areas in which you struggle with this.

- Make a list of the top five influences you can identify.

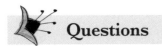 **Questions**

Do I look to friends or social media for validation, or do I consult the Bible first?

Am I swayed by how my culture says I should mother, even if it flies in the face of Scripture?

Am I teaching truth and godly conviction to my children and then practicing it consistently?

 **Prayer**

*Lord, as servants of Christ, we don't want anything that anybody else does to take our eyes off of you. Increase our affections for you and our children each day as we "press on toward the goal to win the prize for which God has called [us] heavenward in Christ Jesus" (Philippians 3:14).*

# 4

# And What Does the Lord Require of Thee?

## SURRENDERING OUR VERSION OF PERFECT MOTHERHOOD TO HIS PERFECT WILL

I grew up attending a variety of churches of various Christian denominations. If anyone ever asked me as a kid if I were a Baptist or a Presbyterian, I probably just squinted at him in confusion. My parents, who are Messianic believers, have always had a heart for the nation of Israel and have even lived there two separate times—once while pregnant with my older brother, who was born there, and once for a year while I was three (then four) and Shae (my brother) was seven. We also attended a charismatic church for a while, and I distinctly remember dancing in the aisles with the other little girls (no falling in a trance or attendants standing by with "modesty coverings" to protect the virtue of any woman so overtaken by the Holy Ghost that she dropped to the floor or anything like that—just lots of joyful exuberance). Since then, I've mostly been involved with nondenominational churches, but we are currently members of a reformed Baptist church.

I'm actually grateful for our smorgasbord approach to the denominations within Christianity because I have experienced firsthand that we are ultimately united in the Body of Christ, not by titles or traditions or habits but by salvation through Christ alone and a mutual love of God and his Holy Word, the Bible. And being aware of the varied ways in which Christians worship is such a beautiful reminder of our uniqueness in Christ. I may not be able to get behind every single practice performed at some churches, but if their core theology is biblically sound, I can worship there. They are my family. (Which is why, if someone ever asks me if I'm a Baptist, I will reply, "No, I'm a Christian.")

## He Has Shown Thee, O Mama

Regardless of which church I've attended, a smattering of familiar "praise songs" (remember when we used to call them that?) have stuck with me through the years. And one of them is Micah 6:8. Raise your hand if you remember doing the women's echoing answer to "Ooo ma-aa-an." If your hand is up, we are church soul sisters, and I just fist-bumped you through these pages. If not, that's cool too. Maybe look the song up anyway. I feel sure there's a YouTube video of it floating around, most likely featuring some Maranatha! Singers sporting impressive mall bangs.

Of course, the best part of the song (besides the echo) is that the lyrics are pure Scripture and come directly from Micah 6:8: "He has shown you, O man, what is good; and what does the LORD require of you but to do justly, to love mercy, and to walk humbly with your God?" (NKJV).

Now, I'm a big believer in the inerrancy of Scripture, so I hope you'll excuse my tweaking this verse just the tiniest bit to this: "He has told you, *O mama*, what is good." I know that "man" is simply a generic term for "human," and I like how the NIV spices it up a bit with the word "mortal." But I don't think it should be lost on us mamas that this verse applies just as much to women and mothers as it does to a man. If there's anyone whose goal should be to "do justice, love kindness, and walk humbly with God," it should be a woman who is in charge of teaching her children to do the same.

The thing is, even though this verse poses one of life's most momentous queries—"what *does* the Lord require of me?"—and then answers it immediately, it's hard not to want God to host a press conference so that we can all ask some follow-up questions.

"What does doing justice look like *for me* as a mother of ten, Lord? Does this just mean that I'm in charge of making sure that everyone gets the same size cookie for dessert?"

"What does it look like for her, a mama of one?"

"Does loving mercy mean letting the little boogers off scot-free every time?"

"Does walking humbly mean that I never share about a great mothering day, in hopes of encouraging some, because it also might make someone else who's struggling feel badly?"

The questions about the *right* way to accomplish these three tasks range from silly to soul-searchingly complex and can cross the eyes and boggle the mind of even the most astute mama.

Unless.

Unless we make a conscious choice to tune out the noise of the world's cultural suggestions, feel-good mantras, and social checklists in favor of the voice of Jesus, who says, "Whoever wants to be my disciple must deny themselves and take up their cross daily and follow me" (Luke 9:23).

I get asked all the time online by fellow mamas how I "make time for myself," how I keep from "losing myself" to motherhood, how I "cope with overwhelm." And I think all of these can be legitimate and necessary questions. Often my answers are purely pragmatic: getting enough sleep, saying no to unnecessary distractions, spending time in God's Word and prayer.

But the wrinkle with each of these questions is that its root is often based in a focus on "me" rather than "he." Colossians 3:23 (ESV) says, "Whatever you do, work heartily, as for the Lord and not for men." Here's the kicker: That part about "men" means "us" too. The prospect of working heartily with the goal of pleasing God, rather than *ourselves*, our neighbors, our mothers, our husbands, our bosses, or anyone else, is a bit of a thorny one. After all, it is God who places us in situations in which we must interact with these people. And we are but humans with very real physical, emotional, and spiritual needs. How are we supposed to pour from an empty cup? If we have not first done that which fulfills *us*, satisfies *us*, pleases *us*, how can we possibly hope to have enough left to offer God or anyone else?

# When We Are Stingy, God Is Generous

Setting aside the backward nature of this question (offering God and others our "leftovers" is never a good idea), let me say this: In the world's economics of motherhood, we can't ever hope to have enough. We will burn out, and even our best intentions will succumb to a selfish, if universal, desire for ease. However, a gospel-centered view of the conundrum asks not "How can *I* if I don't take care of *me* first?" but instead "How will *Christ* in spite of *me*?"

If that sounds a bit too altruistic or fuzzy on the details, let me tell you that this ultra-practical mama of many has seen the miracle of God's grace being sufficient for me and his power being made perfect in my weakness (to paraphrase 2 Corinthians 12:9) in such tangible ways when I have managed to let go of my desire for "the perfect" solution to a problem.

Something you should know about me (that probably won't surprise you, considering my double handful of kids): When I was a teenager, I surrendered to the Lord the exact number of children I would one day have. I remember thinking I might end up with as many as—*gasp*—six!

Ha. There was so much I didn't know.

One thing I did know, though? I wanted the Lord to give me however many kids he had for me one at a time. In other words, I was fully surrendered—as long as God did it my way. Multiples sounded hard. And time-consuming. And impossible. And did I mention hard?

In fact, I was so convinced I had fully given my fertility over to the Lord that I expected him to comply with my "no-twins" policy. (Don't even talk to me about triplets, y'all.) Not that this was a conscious thought. I would have considered that downright sacrilegious. No, it was closer to a subconscious assumption that God's definition of goodness must line up with my own.

So imagine how disconcerting it was to my confidence in my surrendered will to discover in 2012 that I was, in fact, pregnant with identical twins.

The Lord graciously sustained me through that entire pregnancy and even gave me an incredibly peaceful home birth culminating in two perfect baby girls. But his grace didn't stop there. You see, I already had three small children when the twinsies made their debut, and we were in our second year of homeschooling. I didn't have a great plan for how I was going to balance keeping twins alive with schooling my first and second graders and keeping up with a toddler, especially since the twins were due at the beginning of the school year. But I figured if the Lord got me into this "mess," he'd provide a way through it.

As the twins' due date crept ever closer, I prayed a lot about what our school year should look like. I researched several alternative schooling options but received peace about none of them. I had despaired of finding a workable solution for our family and had come to terms with what I'll call a *relaxed* approach to the school year when, mere weeks before the twins were born, some close friends told us that a tiny church-run school close by had decided to offer a hybrid option to homeschoolers. My boys could attend a couple of days a week. The rest of the time would be spent at home, completing the work the school had assigned and pursuing any of our own interests.

Y'all, to say this answer was from the Lord is to downplay the magnitude of the blessing this schooling option proved to be for our family over the next two years. I had figured I would power through somehow, muddle through in some way. And I was right about half of that because there was *plenty* of muddling that first year. One night, I distinctly recall slumping on the floor—a baby clutched in each arm and my other three small children sprawled across various parts of my body—and calling Shaun, who was gone on a work trip. I sobbed incoherently about my filthy floors, mountains of laundry, and utter lack of a dinner plan for that night. I was so dejected that I think he genuinely considered jumping on a plane that second so he could see for himself that the house hadn't collapsed in a shambles.

The Lord's power was made so evident that year in my having nothing to do with that perfectly tailored and oh-so-needed school solution. I didn't make it happen. I just got to stand back and "boast all the more gladly of my weaknesses, so that the power of Christ may rest upon me. For the sake of Christ, then, I am content with weaknesses, insults, hardships, persecutions, and calamities. For when I am weak, then I am strong" (2 Corinthians 12:9-10 ESV).

If I had forced a solution or finagled an outcome to ensure that I didn't "lose my mind," I have no doubt that I, and our family by extension, would have

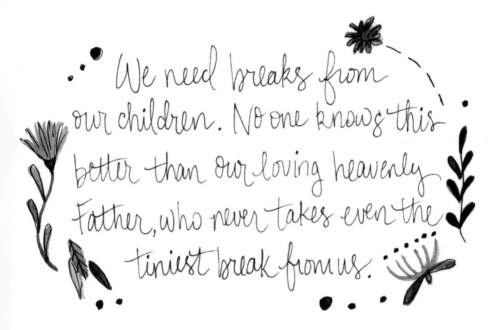

We need breaks from our children. No one knows this better than our loving heavenly Father, who never takes even the tiniest break from us.

experienced more stress, more unrest, and more frustration—not less. There is nothing inherently wrong with making plans (as long as we hold them loosely), nothing wrong with praying for a specific outcome. We need outlets and relief. We need breaks from our children, however brief. But we must remember that no one knows this better than our loving heavenly Father, who never takes even the tiniest break from us. He is the Lord our God who will never leave us or forsake us (Deuteronomy 31:6). And it is only when we rest in the knowledge that his ways are always good (notice I did not say easy) that we are able to truly revel in his provision.

That knowledge is what I rested in when we discovered that our sixth baby (the pregnancy immediately following the Evy and Nola's) was also a twin, and when we discovered we had lost his brother to vanishing twin syndrome at eight weeks. And it was the same knowledge that upheld me when I found out I was expecting twins again, identical boys this time, at thirty-seven years old.

If you started this chapter hoping that I would tell you exactly what kind of mother you should be, I'm afraid I'm going to disappoint you. I don't know your personality, your strengths and weaknesses, your hopes and dreams, your genetics, your background—none of it. But I know the God who does. The God who placed you in the position in which you find yourself for "just such a time as this." The God who prompted you to open and read this book.

And I know this: He will *absolutely* give you more than you can handle—of both joy and pain. He might pile on the trouble so heavily you feel you will suffocate beneath its weight (I've been there). Conversely, he might slather you so thickly with joys and yesses that you're fairly dripping with a goodness you know you don't deserve and could never repay (been there too). Both are blessings. Both are ways that he reveals his callings to us. Both require us to shuffle forward with tiny steps of faith and outstretched palms of gratitude.

*And I know this: He will **absolutely** give you more than you can handle—of both joy and pain.*

If you desire to know God's will for your life as a mother (or anything else), I encourage you to pray a really scary prayer: "Lord, show me what you have for me and then equip me to do it by your power, even if it's nothing like I imagined it would be."

*He has shown you, O mama, what is good and what the Lord requires of you.... It's there, hidden in the mysterious hours of quiet while we nurse our babes, written plainly across the sunlit, wonder-filled faces of our story-rapt toddlers.*

He has shown you, O mama, what is good and what the Lord requires of you. It's in his Word. It's in the daily seeking of him through prayer and petition. It's in the memorizing of Scripture and the constant application of it to our lives. It's in the bottom wiping and the belly laughing, the surprise sonograms and the surly teenagers. It's there, hidden in the mysterious hours of quiet while we nurse our babes, written plainly across the sunlit, wonder-filled faces of our story-rapt toddlers. Moment by moment, day by day, "precept upon precept, line upon line, line upon line, here a little, there a little" (Isaiah 28:10 ESV), we catch glimpses of the ways in which the Lord is molding us into his likeness. There is no shortcut, and there is no generic formula. We must choose to trust in his goodness and be willing to let him tear away at our rough shell until our true skin is revealed, vulnerable and pliable—and bearing the marks of his grace.

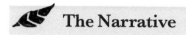

## The Narrative

| MEDIOCRE MOTHERHOOD | CHRISTLIKE MOTHERHOOD |
|---|---|
| Fears the future | Trusts God's plan for the future |
| Resents hardship and struggles | Welcomes adversity for the sake of growth |
| Puts her plans and desires first | Puts God's plans and desires first |

## Action Steps

- Memorize and meditate on Proverbs 3:5-6 (ESV): "Trust in the Lord with all your heart, and do not lean on your own understanding. In all your ways acknowledge him, and he will make straight your paths."

- Identify areas in motherhood that feel scary to you and ask the Lord to help you trust his will in them.

- Pick one exercise of "trusting the Lord" to do with your kids this week.

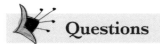 **Questions**

Do I really believe that God's plans for me are better than mine?

Am I willing to do hard or scary things even when the world tells me I would be foolish to do so?

Am I modeling trust in Christ to my children on a daily basis?

 **Prayer**

> *Lord, we know that every good and perfect gift comes from you (James 1:17), and we desire to recognize your goodness in every aspect of our lives. Open our eyes to the ways that you are directing our paths in motherhood so that we can walk boldly in your will.*

# 5

# Self-Care Versus Soul Care

## RECOGNIZING THAT TIME WITH CHRIST IS BETTER THAN "ME TIME"

O f the messages being trumpeted the loudest in our culture (and not just in the arena of motherhood), there are few more insistent than that of the alluring siren of self-care.

She's a marketing genius. And she has saturated practically every form of media from advertising to radio. I can't walk into a coffee shop, turn on the TV, open a magazine, stand in line at the grocery store, or scroll through more than three social media posts without being inundated with suggestions like these:

"You deserve a break."

"Girl, you need..."

"Treat yo' self."

"Whatever makes you happy."

"Prioritize me time."

"It's never wrong if it makes you feel good."

"Self-care is soul care."

There are various problems (from a biblical perspective) with each of these statements. But that last one really trips me up. And not because I completely disagree with it either.

Self-care *can* be soul care. But it matters very much how we define self-care.

And I can tell you right now that almost none of the ways that the above sources categorize self-care will line up with Scripture, which makes it a no-go for me and for any other Christian mama seeking to prioritize the voice of Jesus above even the loudest, most compelling mantras of our current culture.

## Nobody Asked You to Be a Martyr

Before I dive into what Scripture teaches about self-care, I want to say something that I *hope* is obvious but can easily get lost in the shuffle: The opposite of self-care is self-neglect. And self-neglect is never a good thing. We've already talked about Jesus's call to take up your cross daily and follow him. Clearly, Christlike self-denial is a thing. However, devotion to Christ is not the same thing as neglecting your basic needs or choosing to be a "martyr" to the detriment of yourself and your family. *Not* getting enough sleep when you have the option of getting it, *not* taking a shower when you need one, *not* reading a book that would be beneficial and enjoyable to you, *not* exercising when it would improve your mood and health, and you could fit it in—none of these is an example of holiness or godliness.

George Müller, one of the most self-sacrificial men that I have ever read about, understood this. Although he devoted most of his life to caring for the orphans of Bristol, England, ill health sometimes forced him to travel to better climates, far away from his beloved orphans, for extended periods of time. He understood that even though these trips "distracted" him from his primary calling, he would not be able to fulfill this calling at all if he didn't care for his health enough to stay alive.

Self-denial for its own sake is never an antidote to the worldly view of self-care. In fact, intentional self-flagellation (physical or metaphorical) affects us negatively in body and soul. It's just another version of asceticism. This heretical philosophy teaches that the harsher we are on our physical bodies and the more we deny ourselves even some of the simplest pleasures that God has created for us to enjoy, the closer we are to him.

If God intended for us to draw near to him by consistently denying ourselves the goodness with which he has endowed this world, then we certainly wouldn't have verses like "Taste and see that the Lord is good" (Psalm 34:8). Jesus would never have transformed water into the tastiest wine at the wedding. Sex would be a clinical act of reproduction instead of a pleasurable and unifying act of intimacy inside marriage. A God who intended us to ignore our most basic needs and desires would never have dreamt up over 2,000 species of jellyfish to dazzle us or painted the sunset with the most delicate hues of peach against backdrops of vivid tangerine.

We serve a God who created giraffes with their spindly necks, puzzle-piece-patterned bodies, and ludicrously long tongues and called it good. We serve a God who granted newborn babies the most delicious-smelling heads and dreamed up the idea of juicy, sun-warmed strawberries. We serve a God who rejoices over us with singing (Zephaniah 3:17) and thought that the world was incomplete without the contributions of musical geniuses like Handel, Mozart, and Beethoven.

We do *not* serve a curmudgeonly or stingy God but a lavish and loving God, one who delights to give us good gifts, starting with his very presence.

## Making the Effort So That God Can Multiply It

Sadly, we often fail to see this very first gift for the treasure that it is and fall into a habit of striving to replace his peace, "which surpasses all understanding" (Philippians 4:7 ESV), with quick fixes that will never satisfy. I love what my friend Clarita, of the blog *Skies of Parchment*, says about spending time in prayer and Scripture (I'm paraphrasing): "Time with the Lord recharges my batteries. On days that feel too full of everything else to fit in 'me time,' choosing to prioritize time spent with *him* fills me up in a way no other form of self-care could."

It's a bit counterintuitive at first glance. You're saying you *don't* have enough time, and yet you're spending it reading the Bible? But just like he did with the loaves and the fishes, Jesus is faithful to multiply our efforts so that time spent with him is never "wasted" and often amplifies any efforts that follow.

We do not serve a curmudgeonly or stingy God but a lavish & loving God, one who delights to give us good gifts, starting with his very presence.

*Just like he did with the loaves and the fishes, Jesus is faithful to multiply our efforts so that time spent with him is never "wasted" and often amplifies any efforts that follow.*

George Müller (yep, smart guy) once said in response to the claim of being too busy to spend time with God, that four hours of work after an hour of prayer would accomplish more than five hours without prayer.[3] And he was a man who practiced what he preached, spending his entire adult life relying on prayer to communicate his needs to the Lord so clearly that he refused to raise money for his orphanage, trusting instead the promise of Philippians 4:19: "God will supply all your needs according to his riches in glory in Christ Jesus."

Similarly, Martin Luther said, "I have so much to do that I shall spend the first three hours in prayer." Y'all, I can't deny that my first reaction to this declaration is to note that Martin Luther was *not* a mother. The thought of my twin toddlers allowing me even one hour of uninterrupted anything is chuckleworthy. Still, the core truth of his words rings true—the busier we get, the *more* (not less) we need the Lord. Of course, if you're anything like me, the more hectic the day ahead, the more likely you are to skimp on prayer at the outset in hopes that you'll manage to get a whole lot of "praying without ceasing" in *while* being productive.

More often than not, this works out pretty well, actually. I pray for my kids while I treat stains on their laundry, for my husband while I'm scrubbing the bathroom nearest his home office, for my friends while I prep for our workouts, for my whiny attitude while I chop veggies for dinner, and for the state of the world as I compose an Instagram post (every time I get on social media, it seems like the world needs even more prayer than the last). I'm certainly not perfect at it, but I do find that when I am more intentional to "by prayer and supplication with thanksgiving let [my] requests be made known to God" (Philippians 4:6 ESV), I am more grounded, less stressed, more peace-filled, and less entitled.

And my
GOD
will
SUPPLY
all
your
needs
PHILIPPIANS 4:19 CSB

That last word—entitled—is one of the major pitfalls within the self-care movement. I'll address that more in a bit, but first, let me reiterate: We need respite, rest, breaks. It's how we're wired as humans by a God who exemplified this in his incarnate form.

Mark 1:35 says that Jesus "went off to a solitary place, where he prayed."

Mark 3:7 tells us that "Jesus withdrew with his disciples to the lake."

In Matthew 14:13, we learn that "when Jesus heard [that John the Baptist had been beheaded], he withdrew by boat privately to a solitary place."

He even spent forty days alone in the desert. There have been times, especially when both sets of my twins were babies and round-the-clock nursing was beginning to take its toll, that a forty-day solo trip to the desert hasn't sounded too bad. Jesus's total abstinence from snacks is problematic, though. Man may not live by bread alone, but nursing mamas need carbs!

But I digress.

My point is that Jesus knew the value of time spent alone with his Father. But he also knew the value of his earthly ministry, and he poured out his patience and giftings on those who needed him. Even when he desired—nay, craved—solitude, he did not treat it as something to which he was entitled (there's that word again). Because there's a difference between wanting (or even needing) and *deserving*.

In Mark 7, Jesus tries to enter a house without anyone knowing about it. Word gets out, though, and soon a Gentile woman is pleading with him to heal her daughter. Does Jesus hold tightly to his right to alone time? Nope. He heals the woman's little girl.

The rest of that Matthew 14 passage from above reveals that even amid his grief over his cousin's death, "when Jesus landed and saw a large crowd, he had compassion on them and healed their sick." I don't know about you, but I would have probably marched the other way, citing burnout and an urgent need for "me time."

Think about all the times that you've thought something akin to "I just want to pee alone. That's not too much to ask, right, Lord?" Or "I just want to go ten minutes without being touched. Just. Ten. Minutes."

I can't help but think that Jesus must have felt similarly when he "saw the crowd around him" and "gave orders to cross to the other side of the lake. Then a teacher of the law came to him and said, 'Teacher, I will follow you wherever you go'" (Matthew 8:18-19). I genuinely wonder if Jesus thought, "Please don't."

Or how about all those times we read about the "crowds pressing in around him"? If anybody should have been over being touched, it was Jesus. In fact, when the woman with the chronic bleeding reaches out for Jesus and is healed, and Jesus notices, his disciples respond incredulously, "You see the people crowding against you...and yet you can ask, 'Who touched me?'" (Mark 5:31). I distinctly remember instances of reading aloud to my children while pregnant with my twin boys and with a toddler on my lap, a five-year-old wedged into the chair beside me, and my twin girls, perched on the arms of the chair, leaning on me or twirling my hair. Between the babies jostling in my womb and the profusion of little limbs surrounding me, I couldn't have told you *whose* elbow was jammed into my ribs the most. And yet I still didn't have hundreds of people desperately scrabbling at me in hopes of healing.

I am all for leaping at the chance for any moments of rest that present themselves. Denying ourselves such gifts is pure foolishness and leads to burnout. Jesus understood this. It's why he took great pains to prioritize the true self-care of soul care with the Father.

 *Jesus took great pains to prioritize the true self-care of soul care with the Father.*

However.

He never adopted an attitude of bitterness or resentment when his plans were "foiled" by the neediness of, well, everybody.

And that, dear friends, is quite the tricky line to walk. After all, Jesus was God. And man, yes. But a sinless man. So what hope do I, a sinful woman, have of emulating his perfect example? The answer is no hope at all without the transforming power of the Holy Spirit—a transformation that is only possible when I prioritize soul care over self-care.

But grace—grace that is greater than all my sin, including misplaced priorities.

Even when we are not perfect in our pursuit of God—which, let's be honest, is always—even when our priorities have been derailed thanks to life circumstances such as pregnancy, sleepless nights, job stresses, marital discord, or fractious kids, God is gracious to provide us with times of refreshment that minister to both our physical and spiritual needs. How do I know this? Because I'm typing this while sitting in my favorite local Vietnamese restaurant as my mom wrangles my kids at home. We hire her to do so, and it is money well spent because it is such a cup-filling experience to sneak away for a few hours to write in an interruption-free environment.

*Even when we are not perfect in our pursuit of God—which, let's be honest, is always— God is gracious to provide us with times of refreshment that minister to both our physical and spiritual needs.*

It is self-care and soul care—because the two truly don't have to be mutually exclusive. I am able to pray over these words as the Lord gives them to me, ask for his guidance when I get stuck, praise him for perfectly crisp and salty sweet potato fries and juicy banh mi. These moments of alone time with the Lord, my laptop, and delicious food are a privilege, *not* something that I deserve. I can write at home, and I often do, sneaking in snatches here and there between homeschooling and prepping dinner. I enjoy those times too. But it is the very recognition that the freedom to write unencumbered from time to time is a gift, rather than my due, that increases my appreciation for it.

# An Attitude of Gratitude (It's Not Just a Platitude)

And therein, my friends, lies the rub. Does self-care—whatever that looks like—produce an attitude of gratitude in us? Or do we begin to expect such privileges on the regular, even to the point of pouting when we can't have them? An indignant reader once interpreted my statement that we do not "deserve" a pedicure as shaming anyone who wanted one—something I wouldn't do, since I myself enjoy pedicures. Her reaction only underscores how touchy we can get when our entitlement is threatened.

What I had actually said was that there was nothing wrong with wanting a pedicure as long as we weren't so attached to the prospect that our happiness depended on it, or we threw a hissy fit if we couldn't have one.

Maybe pedicures aren't your thing. Maybe it's an hour at the gym to read a good book on the treadmill while your kids are in childcare. Maybe it's a yearly trip to a "big city" with a friend to celebrate a birthday. Maybe it's making a fancy meal from scratch without anyone tugging on your elbow. Maybe it's gardening.

Different things will reenergize different people. And many things that bring us joy and rest—even the seemingly frivolous ones—do so because the Lord has designed us in such a way as to enjoy them to their fullest. They are one small part of "every good and perfect gift [that] is from above, coming down from the Father of the heavenly lights, who does not change like shifting shadows" (James 1:17).

The real trick is learning how to truly appreciate those moments of gifted goodness, without making them into an idol, *while* prioritizing time with the Gift-Giver. Do we live for wine o'clock, or do we thirst for the life-giving water that Jesus offered the Samaritan woman at the well in John 4? Do we count down the days to the weekend, when we can sleep in just a little, or do we carve out fifteen minutes of quiet time with the Father to start our days whenever possible? Thankfully, we have Jesus as our model in this as in everything. What if the next time we heard the phrase "treat yo' self," we immediately thought of Christ's words instead:

What father among you, if his son asks for a fish, will give him a snake instead? Or if he asks for an egg, will give him a scorpion? So if you who are evil know how to give good gifts to your children, how much more will your Father in heaven give the Holy Spirit to those who ask Him! (Luke 11:11-13 BSB).

The Lord cares about us. He desires good things for us. He already has our best interests at heart. We are graven on his palms (Isaiah 49:16), and our tears are individually written in his record book (Psalm 56:8). When we grasp at our culture's version of self-care as the ultimate remedy for our woes, we discount the fact that the very God of the universe was the one who gave us a love for really good books or bubble baths. We miss the fact that both our souls and our physical selves are in his tender care every moment of every day.

And no other care can compare with that.

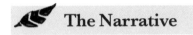 ## The Narrative

| MEDIOCRE MOTHERHOOD | CHRISTLIKE MOTHERHOOD |
| --- | --- |
| Performs self-care with a focus on self | Performs self-care with a focus on soul |
| Says you can't pour from an empty cup | Says, in Christ, "my cup runneth over" |
| Feels entitled to "me time" | Feels grateful for even short breaks |

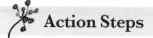

## Action Steps

- Memorize and meditate on Philippians 4:19 (ESV): "And my God will supply every need of yours according to his riches in glory in Christ Jesus."

- Commit to spending time in the soul care of prayer and reading God's Word three times this week.

- Choose and do one self-care activity (a shower, a workout, ten pages of a good book...) that brings joy and helps you to serve your family better.

## Questions

Am I using self-care as an excuse for self-indulgence?

Conversely, am I denying myself basic needs in the name of "taking up my cross," even though it's detrimental to my health and makes me a less effective mother?

How can my kids and I choose soul care together this week?

## Prayer

*Lord, you already know what we need before we ask (Matthew 6:8), but you still desire that we come to you to be filled with your presence. Keep us focused on caring for our souls with your Word and prayer, trusting that you will supply everything else we need because you love us so well.*

# When We're Guilty of Mom Guilt

## LEARNING THE DIFFERENCE BETWEEN SHAME AND HOLY SPIRIT CONVICTION

I have a confession that may shock some of you, given my many-kids status. Ready?

I don't drink coffee. (I'll give you a minute to let that sink in.)

Not only do I not imbibe, but I actively dislike the taste *and* smell of the stuff. I know: how bizarre. Once, when Starbucks was offering some sort of chemically laden but scrumptious seasonal syrup, I ordered my "usual" for those rare times that I find myself in a coffee shop: hot chocolate, extra hot, with whip. (This is my attempt to *look* like an adult while satisfying the cravings of my inner ten-year-old.) Except this time I added a shot of that yummy syrup. There were a lot of flavors competing in that little cup of sugar, but I took one tiny sip and immediately scrunched my face in distaste. I handed it to my coffee-adoring best friend and said, "Try this. There's coffee in it."

She took a sip and shook her head. "Nope. No coffee in there."

But there was, and I knew it. I took my cup back to the barista and asked if he had, by chance, added java, and he realized he had. *That's* how strong a coffee aversion I have.

I have been asked so many times where I find energy, given my lack of regular caffeine intake, and the answer is going to downright annoy some of you: To some extent, I just have it. I attribute some of it to a decent (though far from pristine) diet and lots of exercise. I'm also an avid fan of power naps. I can claim neither a completely consistent sleep schedule (said every mother ever) nor "legal addictive stimulants" (to quote Joe from *You've Got Mail*). And yet energy is a must because, once our day starts, there are too many people and things that need my attention for me to drag around like a zombie. And so I have had to train myself to do the next thing, even when I don't particularly feel like it.

## Escaping the Whirlpool of Condemnation

Do not, for one moment, imagine that I am some sort of machine who powers through every moment of exhaustion with a *Stepford Wives* grin on my face. But I have learned that doing hard things, tedious things, needful things, is, in itself, a reward at times. Because "done" things don't come back to bite you like "undone" ones. There's only a very limited amount of ignoring the dirty clothes hamper I can do before it threatens to swallow the laundry room whole. And then I'm liable to start in on a cycle of "Why did you do that to yourself? Now you have to play catch up for days. What were you thinking?" These days, I would much rather do something when I'm tired than skip it and spend two energy-draining hours beating myself up over the fact that I didn't just get it done.

*"Mom guilt" is applicable only if we are actually guilty of the mud our own brains are slinging at us.*

Having received dozens of reader emails about "mom guilt," I know I'm not the only one who can get trapped in that whirlpool of self-condemnation.

It took years of fighting and praying against that voice in my head telling me I wasn't "doing enough" before I could fully internalize a couple of simple but life-altering truths:

1. "Mom guilt" is applicable only if we are actually guilty of the mud our own brains are slinging at us.
2. God is way more interested in our holiness than a daily litany of our shortcomings (although he is so kind and patient with us when we do vent our frustrations).

I have had days when I wake up early, teach my weight-training class, come home, feed my kids a nutritious breakfast, and then proceed to churn my way through homeschooling, emails, making food, nursing babies, reading to toddlers, housecleaning, giving my husband attention, and even texting my friends back in a somewhat timely manner, only to berate myself for having "failed" when I fall into bed, exhausted, at 11:00 p.m. with five things left undone on "my list."

That's unwarranted mom guilt right there, plain and simple.

I have also had days when I spend too much time on my phone, distracted by social media or trying to track down the best price on a rug for the dining room. My kids get my fractured attention, dinner is haphazard, and I crawl into bed feeling scattered and guilty that I have not done my best. And you know what? I'm right. That guilt—or Holy Spirit conviction, rather—is warranted because I truly did not approach my profession of motherhood with excellence "as for the Lord" (Colossians 3:23 ESV) that day.

## I Am Not the Captain of This Ship

The common denominator between these two scenarios is a convicting one. In neither situation have I done a good job of committing my way to the Lord (Psalm 37:5) at the outset of my day. When I wake up and hit the ground, road-runner legs whirling, without first taking the time to ask the Lord to ground my focus on his plans for my life that day, I am more prone to view my final "performance" through the critical eye of a perfectionist. On the other hand, when

AS

FAR

AS

THE

EAST

IS

FROM

THE WEST

PSALM 103:12

I neglect to first ask the Lord for focus and discipline to accomplish my tasks well, I am capable of letting my interests govern me rather than the other way around. (Remember that George Müller quote about accomplishing more in four hours with one hour of prayer than in five without it?)

The fact is that there is no biblical precedent for our being "enough" in our own strength. Instead, one of the most well-loved verses in Scripture commands us to "trust in the Lord with all your heart and lean not on your own understanding. In all your ways submit to him, and he will direct your paths" (Proverbs 3:5-6).

Making the conscious choice to trust in the Lord for my day-to-day tasks takes the pressure of a performance-focused mindset out of the equation. I no longer view myself as the captain of my ship, and my worth is no longer defined by the number of boxes I check. Not only that, but when life inevitably interferes with my plans, I can rest assured that this too can work together for my good (Romans 8:28). When we internalize the truth that God is the one directing our paths, those unexpected twenty minutes spent crawling around looking for a missing toddler shoe *with* said toddler are no longer simply an obstacle to our productivity. Instead, it is a time full of a purpose that can only be granted it by an omniscient and loving God who is more concerned with growing our patience and empathy (because we misplace shoes too) than our to-do lists. It is also an opportunity to "in every situation, by prayer and petition, with thanksgiving, present your requests to God" (Philippians 4:6). I have lost count of how many times I have hunted for a particularly elusive item only to finally realize that I have yet to stop and ask God to help me find it, and then, when I do, have lifted a cushion to discover it within arm's reach.

## Shedding the Cape of Complete Competence

Maybe you feel guilty because you worry you're not splitting your time evenly between your children.

Maybe you feel guilty because your child is sick, and you wonder what you could have done to prevent it.

Maybe you feel guilty because you lost your temper again.

Maybe you feel guilty because you don't really enjoy the stage your kid is in.

Maybe you feel guilty because you're in a season of overwhelm, and you just can't seem to "do it all" like you once did.

Maybe you feel guilty because your kids don't get to do as many activities as their peers.

Maybe you feel guilty because you don't get as much accomplished in a day as your neighbor, Becky.

(These are, by the way, actual worries expressed by actual readers whom I polled about this topic.)

Here's the truth: "As far as the east is from the west, so far has he removed our transgressions from us" (Psalm 103:12).

Also: "If we confess our sins, he is faithful and just and will forgive us our sins and purify us from all unrighteousness" (1 John 1:9).

In addition: "Your love has delivered me from the pit of oblivion, for You have cast all my sins behind Your back" (Isaiah 38:17 BSB).

The good news is that although we are *all* born under the curse of sin and death, Christ took the full brunt of that curse on himself on the cross. Our debt is fully covered. We stand guiltless before the throne of grace.

Hallelujah, right?

So why are we sometimes so beset with mom guilt? And about things over which we often have little control?

First, as I mentioned above, we often feel guilty because we are assuming a mantle of responsibility that was never ours to wear: the Cape of Complete Competence. We are charging through our days with the assumption that God couldn't possibly care about our mundanities—which means we must ace them on our own—when Scripture makes it very clear that he cares about every unwashed hair on our dry-shampooed heads. When I consistently commit my ways (all of them) to the Lord, that heavy mantle slips from my shoulders, and I am able to stand erect in the confidence of Christ's "enoughness."

Second, when we fail to invite the Lord into every aspect of our daily grind, we leave ourselves open to Satan's attack. As 1 Peter 5:8 says, "Be alert and of sober mind. Your enemy the devil prowls around like a roaring lion looking for

Scripture makes it very clear that God cares about every unwashed hair on our dry-shampooed heads.

someone to devour." Lucifer would love nothing better than to plump us up with lies of false condemnation and then gobble us whole. He can't take our salvation away, but he can steal our peace if we let him. He is the "father of lies" (John 8:44), and he loves nothing better than tangling us up in a web of shame and self-focus.

Lie: "You're always late."

Truth: "I have been late several times recently because my three-year-old is especially challenging right now, and it's more important to take the time to lovingly address his tantrums than to simply yank him out the door so we can be on time. I'll plan ahead better next week."

Lie: "You will never stop losing your temper."

Truth: "I am struggling with patience right now, but I can repent of that and be forgiven. I am no longer a slave to sin (Romans 6)."

Lie: "She's killing it, and you're barely getting by. You will never measure up."

Truth: "She needs God's grace just as much as I do, and even when I am not 'wise by human standards,' God chooses the 'weak things of the world to shame the strong' (1 Corinthians 1:27). There is hope for me yet."

I could go on, but my point is that we believe even the most outlandish untruths when we are not grounded in God's Word. There is no better cure for deceit than the medicine of Scripture.

Third, until we get to heaven, we will continue to fall short of God's glory every day. Dismissing all mom guilt as "Satan's lies" or "society's unrealistic expectations" can mask the truth that we really are guilty of the thing the Holy Spirit is whispering in our ears. Second Corinthians 13:5 (ESV) says to "examine yourselves, to see whether you are in the faith. Test yourselves. Or do you not realize this about yourselves, that Jesus Christ is in you?"

If Jesus is in us, there is no fear in truthful self-examination. For "if God is for us, who can be against us?" (Romans 8:31). We can acknowledge areas for improvement without sinking into despair. We can receive the timely admonishment of a friend without defensiveness. We can address blind spots without letting them define our worth.

It's kind of like that coffee-tinged hot chocolate I mentioned earlier. I know many of you will think it nothing short of sacrilege to compare your favorite drink to sin, but when we truly abhor something enough to recognize it for what it is right away, we won't be able to tolerate it, even in small amounts. May we be so in tune with God's standards of holiness that we truly "hate what is evil" and "cling to what is good" (Romans 12:9). May we be grateful for that pang of genuine conviction that helps us to repent quickly and completely of whatever is stealing our affections from Christ.

The culture of mediocre motherhood will tell us that mom guilt is (take your pick) society's, men's, or our mom's tool to control us and that we should ignore it because we are perfect just the way we are. The Bible tells us that "there is no one righteous, not even one" (Romans 3:11), but despite that, nothing "can separate us from the love of God that is in Christ Jesus," and we are "more than conquerors through him who loved us" (Romans 8:37-39).

The worldly approach represents a flimsy and false foundation of bravado, which *will* crumble in the face of sleepless nights, hormonal swings, and "bad days." The biblical approach promises freedom from circumstantial control in favor of daily growth and sanctification.

I don't know about you, but I'd rather live in freedom every day of the week.

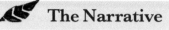 

| MEDIOCRE MOTHERHOOD | CHRISTLIKE MOTHERHOOD |
|---|---|
| Calls all forms of guilt unhealthy | Acknowledges that we are guilty of sin |
| Opts for an empty gospel of self-love | Glories in the gospel of Christ's completed work on the cross |
| Finds worth in results alone | Chooses contentment in Christ |

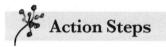 **Action Steps**

- Memorize and meditate on Romans 8:1 (ESV): "There is therefore now no condemnation for those who are in Christ Jesus."

- Make a list of three lies Satan wants you to believe about your mothering, and then find the truth in Scripture.

- Ask the Lord to reveal one area of genuine Holy Spirit conviction and how to address it.

 **Questions**

Am I allowing false mom guilt to keep me trapped in condemnation?

On the other hand, am I ignoring areas that need to be addressed because I'm believing the world's "perfect just the way you are" mantra?

What is one way I can model being in tune with the Holy Spirit this week to my children?

**Prayer**

> *Lord, you have separated our sins from us as far as the east is from the west (Psalm 103:12), and you are gracious to convict us when our mothering doesn't look like what Scripture teaches. Strengthen our wills to resist Satan's lies of condemnation, and soften our hearts to accept the Holy Spirit's nudges of conviction.*

# The Profession of Motherhood

## EMBRACING OUR PRIMARY CALLING
## IN THE FACE OF CULTURAL DISDAIN

My best friend and I own an art print business together, and during its infancy, what seemed like a golden opportunity fell into our laps. We were invited to offer little bundles of our prints as part of a swag bag for each table at an event that featured several Christian "powerhouse" women. We were so excited! I only recognized two of the names on the panel, and while I knew I probably wouldn't completely agree with the sentiments of the one I had heard the most about, it wasn't an issue of heresy. And it *was* a great business connection, not to mention an excuse to get away for a girls' weekend.

We feverishly prepared our goodies and then set out on a road trip of several hours with a couple of other girls, laughing, chattering, and stopping too many times for coffee (Dr. Pepper Icees for me). The event was sold out, and it looked like the stuff of every Instagram-savvy (there were many "influencers" in the audience), Pinterest-loving girl's dream. There were twinkle lights, hand-lettered rustic wooden table markers, white chairs against a green lawn, soft music, and yummy food.

It *should* have been a night to remember. And in many ways it was—just not for the reasons I was hoping. In fact, as the panel discussion began, I felt my buoyant mood deflate. I don't remember the exact title of the topic, but the basic gist was "balancing motherhood and profession."

## "I Am a Mama"

All the women on the panel had full-time freelance careers. In other words, they were their own bosses and managed their own time while producing their various wares (books, shopping websites, jewelry, and the like). They freely acknowledged this autonomy threw a significant wrench in things like child-care, regular hours, and general family/job balance.

Now, before you get your knickers in a twist, please understand that this is not a chapter about the pros and cons of the motherhood side hustle. I teach fitness classes. I blog, write books, and budget time for social media. I have that art print business I mentioned. Clearly, I have no issues with doing things that produce income and require skills beyond those inherent to motherhood. (And you would be hard-pressed to find any indictment of industrious womanhood in Scripture, especially when you look at the Proverbs 31 woman and her house-hold-managing, garment-producing, property-buying bad self.) However, if you were to ask me my *profession*, as a homeschooling mama who spends 90 percent of most days with my kids, I would say, without hesitation, "I am a mama."

Not only were the women on this panel all mothers, but all of them had at least three children. Two had five. They were MOMs (remember: Moms of Many) by Western standards. This does not make anyone any more or less of a mother than someone with fewer or more children, but in the eyes of our culture, the more children one has, the more strongly the correlation between identity and motherhood seems to emerge. And yet I doubt that any of these talented, articulate, ambitious women would have claimed motherhood as their profession. And the reason I doubt that is because of their own bits of advice that they passed out with both authority and what often bordered on disdain.

"Ain't nobody got time for that" (referring to toddler interruptions during working hours).

"Don't get me wrong—I love my children, but thank GAWD for public education, or I would never get any real work done."

"I am my own boss. I refuse to feel guilty for being a darn good one. I have employees that need me."

"I know my kids are proud of me for how hard I work. They will understand one day when they have their own jobs."

They touched on subjects like extracurricular activities (they made some really good points), mom guilt (which they dismissed as the invention of a patriarchal society), and the "light at the end of the tunnel" (which I'll address in a second).

As I listened, I noticed a distinct lack of biblical backing for most of their points, many of which, though sometimes helpful in a practical way, were firmly rooted in popular modern cultural mores about women and motherhood. Many of their comments bore an eerie resemblance to those attitudes of either apathy or defiance that I defined as "mediocre" in my first chapter, even though none of these women would *ever* qualify as mediocre by "hustle culture" standards.

The longer they spoke, the more disconnected I felt, and yet, as I glanced around, I noticed something that piqued my interest. Most of the women at the event were young, attractive "go-getters," and they were lapping up the advice these slightly older, attractive "go-getters" were doling out as if it were the life-giving water that Jesus offered the Samaritan woman at the well.

And understandably so.

The speakers were engaging—magnetic, even. They were witty, well-spoken, and extremely successful. They already represented the pinnacle of Christian women's achievements. Most of them have gone on to become exponentially more so, morphing from small-time social media celebrities into influential household names with millions of acolytes and multimillions in book sales.

Dishearteningly, several of them have since veered away from biblical Christianity entirely, choosing instead to promote a version of Jesus that doesn't exist within the pages of Scripture and to make bold statements about issues that fly in the face of crystal clear Bible teachings.

As I sat listening, processing, observing, and feeling the pricking of Holy Spirit conviction, I couldn't help but acknowledge that outside of a solid grounding in Scripture, I might have found the version of motherhood they were peddling just as appealing as many of my neighbors.

## The (Dim) Light at the End of the Tunnel

Even so, I couldn't help but wince when the leader of the panel drove home the final point—that "light at the end of the tunnel" that I mentioned earlier.

"I know many of you have dreams in your heart," she said. "God put those dreams there. And he created you for a specific purpose. He knows your drive and passion. He knows how much you yearn to spread your wings and fly into the purpose he made just for you. But he also gave you these sweet kiddos, and they are only with you all the time for a short while, even though it may feel like a long time. So hang in there, mamas. Your time is coming. Before you know it, your kids will be heading off to kindergarten, and you'll finally be free to lean into your God-given calling. You will not be 'just' a bottom wiper or a bedtime story reader forever. *Your time will come.*"

I understood exactly what she meant. I wrote a novel (which shall forever remain unpublished, amen) when I was twenty-four years old and was busy teaching Spanish part-time and taking care of my first baby. And then, the next year, when I had two very small children to care for, I spent every free moment shopping that novel around to agents and researching the publishing process. This was all while we were building our first DIY home, so the "free" moments were few, and I can remember feeling frustrated to have just waded into my daily list of email contacts only to hear my six-month-old begin to fuss himself awake from his usual naptime much too early.

I had a "dream in my heart" to write a book. But God had also given me "these sweet kiddos." What to do?

The more I thought it over, prayed about it, and read my Bible, the more I realized that I had that order backward. God had given me the extraordinary privilege of raising up children for his purposes and his glory, *and* in addition (not in precedence), he had given me a dream of writing and publishing a book. It took more than a dozen years—nine of which I spent blogging and honing my voice and focus—and *eight* more kids before *he* (not I) saw fit to orchestrate all the circumstances that would allow those two dreams to coexist.

Ultimately, my problem with that panel leader's exhortation was not that I didn't understand its appeal. The problem was that I knew its appeal all too well, and I knew it to be one that promised big results but delivered mostly frustration. The constant friction from trying to "balance" my professions of mother and writer rubbed my emotions raw. It produced resentment for my own children when I couldn't get my writing work done when I wanted to. And then, of course, I felt guilty for resenting them.

It wasn't until I stopped struggling to carve my time up into neat, equal compartments of work and motherhood that I was able to finally achieve what I can only describe as a God-given sense of peace and, yes, relief.

When I embraced "Mama" as my profession, the rest of my interests largely fell into place. Notice I did not say that they simply disappeared. I continued to write and even started a blog when my third baby was seven months old. I published a post on that blog five days a week for almost a year (insane), and during that time, the Lord nudged me to recalibrate my focus multiple times. Near the end of that first year, I found out I was pregnant with Evy and Nola, and the Lord made it abundantly clear that I needed to pull back and recenter yet again. I'm so grateful he did, not only because I have my sweet Evangeline and Magnolia as a result of it, but also because I would have had a harder time keeping my "professional" focus on target without my circumstances requiring it. My blog was growing quickly, and the temptation to prioritize all the strangers clamoring for my attention over my own family was strong at times.

## Finding the Right Kind of Attagirl

The truth about motherhood as a profession is that it can be a bit of a thankless one, especially when our kids are very young. In a traditional workplace, the boss passes out "employee of the month" awards. Or she dangles a Christmas bonus in front of our noses to motivate us. My toddlers have dangled a variety of objects in my face at times, but most of them have been slimy, and none have remotely resembled dollar bills (unless they've been digging through my purse again).

Or maybe, if we are our own bosses, we reward *ourselves* with a "treat" when we have reached a certain goal. One of the authors on that panel said that once she achieved a certain career objective, she treated herself to a trip to Oprah's favorite spa, an experience that had been on her professional bucket list for years. In her eyes, this trip meant she had "made it."

So how do we keep trudging along through the trenches of largely anonymous motherhood without losing heart? (I'm not saying motherhood always feels like a slog, but it can.) How do we know when we've "made it"? After all, everybody needs an "attagirl" every now and then, right?

The short answer to this is a resounding yes. But the longer answer is a bit more complex.

If we truly believe that we cannot continue to do good work without recognition, we will often find ourselves disappointed. Maybe our husband won't notice that we mopped for the first time in months, and it will get us in a funk about what an unappreciative lout he is. Or Aunt Mildred will make another passive-aggressive comment about how much better so-and-so is at keeping her kids looking decent (hint: She's probably saying the same thing to so-and-so), even though we have been making a monumental effort to run a hairbrush through the tangles every day while keeping our own personal laundry Vesuvius from erupting.

The truth is, "People look at the outward appearance, but the Lord looks at the heart" (1 Samuel 16:7). Our sparkling floors and pristine French braids mean very little if our hearts are full of irritation at not having our best efforts noticed. On the other hand, when we choose excellence in motherhood (*however* the Lord has revealed that to us, because this can look very different from a perpetually clean house and tidy hair), we *always* have an "attagirl" waiting for us in the pages of Scripture.

In Ephesians 6:7-8 (ESV), Paul exhorts slaves to render "service with a good will as to the Lord and not to man, knowing that whatever good anyone does, this he will receive back from the Lord, whether he is a bondservant or is free."

Our professional standards of excellence start at home with the people who live under our own roofs.

We know from Romans 6 (and many other passages) that we are "slaves to Christ" in the best possible way, which means that this act of working for God's rather than "man's" approval applies to everyone. And it comes with the promise of a return of good from the Lord: the best kind of "attagirl" there is.

Not only that, but we have a biblical model in Titus 2 for surrounding ourselves with the kind of women who will encourage us in our goal of "killing it" in the profession of motherhood. Sometimes it's hard to find that kind of wisdom in person (I've already talked about how I prayed for this kind of mentorship for years before the Lord brought along several women who were willing to pour their wisdom and encouragement into my life), but that's what books, podcasts, and blogs are for. (I mean, I'm sure glad Ruth had Naomi because she certainly didn't have access to all the resources that you and I do.) Above all, that's what the Bible is for.

## High Professional Standards Start at Home

Opportunities to encourage and be encouraged in motherhood abound, but so do distractions. So does comparison. So do "selfish ambition" and "vain conceit" (Philippians 2:3). After all, what if motherhood just isn't my jam? What if that's not where I get my primary validation? What if I really feel like I was called to something different, greater, higher?

I'm about to ruffle some serious feathers by saying this, but I'll tell it to you straight: If you already *are* a mother, then no other profession you can claim during your primary season of mothering can trump that of your job as a mama. Why? Because nothing else has the potential to impact the everlasting souls of the precious humans who have been entrusted to you (and to no one else) as much as the act of worship that is laying aside your other interests to focus on loving your family well.

*If you already are a mother, then no other profession you can claim during your primary season of mothering can trump that of your job as a mama.*

This is not to say that motherhood is the highest calling there is. It isn't. Singleness can be just as sacred. Childlessness can be just as God-honoring. If you are a woman and you are not a mother, you are not diminished in capacity or worth.

However, if we *are* already mothers and we are not prioritizing that job, someone is suffering as a result. (Hint: It's us *and* our kids.) Not only that, but we are shortchanging our profession of motherhood in a way we (hopefully) never would in any other area of our lives. When I see "mediocre motherhood" memes about surviving kids by day drinking or by hiding in the closet eating a pack of Oreos while your offspring run wild, I can't help but wonder if this is the same way this person approaches her "real" job. And I ask myself, "What if I showed up late for work all the time? Dressed inappropriately for the position? Paid lax attention when my coworkers are speaking? Responded rudely when addressed? Complained constantly? Indulged in frequent sarcasm? Belittled my boss?"

The answer: I sure wouldn't be getting pegged for employee of the month. And rightfully so. I'm not giving my profession its due as unto the Lord—or even as unto some basic standards of human decency.

So why do we joke about letting ourselves get away with things in motherhood that we never would if an earthly boss were watching (*especially* in light of a heavenly Father who is)? Partly because of that "lack of recognition" thing I mentioned before. Partly because of the never-ending nature of motherhood's demands (there's no such thing as "knocking off" for the day at five). Partly because we can easily believe the lie that motherhood, of all professions, is the least legitimate. And partly because we have not trained ourselves to choose

YOU ARE SERVING THE **LORD CHRIST**

COLOSSIANS 3:24 ESV

hard things and to see the value in investing *now* to produce long-term fruit in ourselves and our children.

 *We must not lose sight of the precious opportunity for eternal impact that sleeps so sweetly in our toddler's bed (even when he gets out of it every other night so he can come pee in ours).*

I have now had the opportunity to be the one giving advice to young mothers from a speaking panel, and this is what I tell them: Our professional standards start at home with the people who live under our own roofs. How we prioritize their needs and the attitudes we cultivate toward them speak volumes about how we define excellence in any area. Our children notice when we resent them or treat them as second skimmings. Far from being "proud" of us for pursuing professions that dominate our attention, our kids internalize our prioritizing career over them as a form of rejection, and they respond in a variety of negative ways. We cannot fall victim to the lie that an attitude of apathy or dismissal in motherhood will not bleed into every other aspect of our lives. And we must not lose sight of the precious opportunity for eternal impact that sleeps so sweetly in our toddler's bed (even when he gets out of it every other night so he can come pee in ours).

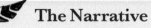 **The Narrative**

| MEDIOCRE MOTHERHOOD | CHRISTLIKE MOTHERHOOD |
|---|---|
| Scoffs at motherhood as a profession | Views the profession of motherhood as a high and holy calling |
| Assumes that mothering is marking time until we can do something really important | Sees time spent with kids as an investment in eternity |
| Underestimates the impact on our kids of prioritizing career over children | Chooses excellence in motherhood first |

 **Action Steps**

- Memorize and meditate on Colossians 3:23-24 (ESV): "Whatever you do, work heartily, as for the Lord and not for men, knowing that from the Lord you will receive the inheritance as your reward. You are serving the Lord Christ."

- List five things that you can do to improve professionally as a mother, and then pick one to focus on this week.

- Ask your kids for ways that you can serve them better (be prepared to be humbled!).

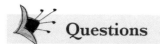

## Questions

Do I truly approach motherhood as a profession at which to excel every day?

Am I more excited by the concept of having my kids "out of my hair" or by the prospect of raising up eternal souls for Christ's kingdom?

Do I believe that I, first and foremost, have been tasked with the primary privilege of training up my kids to love God?

## Prayer

*Lord, you know that we grow weary of the ceaselessness of the profession of motherhood. Help us to truly recognize its worth in a culture that values it little. Help us to do even the little things "as for you," knowing that we are serving Christ and our children in the process.*

# When the Seat of Our Pants Tears

## LEARNING THE ART OF SELF-DISCIPLINE

Y ou know that verse in the Bible that talks about training up a child in the way he should go (Proverbs 22:6 ESV)?

It's a good one, right?

And it even comes with a rock-solid principle (I love it when they do that!): "When he is old, he will not depart from it."

Notice that it doesn't mention what our children will do when they are young or middle-aged. I know too many mamas who bank on that promise being an instant one and are disappointed when they don't see the fruit of their labor right away or all the time. But I encounter even more mamas who were not themselves trained up in the way they should go, and as a result, do not really know where to start with their own kids. They tell me that the concept of child training seems solid, but the application feels a little slippery.

Here is just a smattering of the questions that I get asked about child training:

"How do you deal with whining? It's gotten so bad that I want to crawl under my covers and hide."

"How do I encourage my seven-year-old to help with a cheerful heart?"

"How do I keep my toddlers in their own beds? I am so sleep-deprived!"

"How can I encourage my twelve-year-old to be self-directed and notice when things need doing?"

"How do I get my four-year-old to poop on the potty?"

## We've Got Some Training to Do

I plan to share what kernels of wisdom I have gleaned from Scripture, fellow mamas, and my own experiences in these areas soon, but first let me say this: Chances are if you're wondering these or similar things, then you've probably got some training to do. (I can't help but hear Ricky Ricardo's voice telling Lucy she's got some "'splainin' to do.") And not of your kids only but of yourself as well.

I know I sure did as a twenty-five-year-old mama of a headstrong, sensitive two-year-old firstborn who felt things deeply and expressed those feelings with great vigor.

I'm the youngest of two. My experience with small children was laughably limited. I had zero practice in how to sleep train a baby, regulate a toddler tantrum, or establish a good bedtime routine. What I did have, by the grace of God, was an excellent mother who had modeled self-control and patient discipline as she raised me. I also have a stubborn streak, which to this day makes me loathe to give up once I've dived into something hard. That tenacity seemed to serve me well when we decided to potty train our oldest shortly after he turned two. It was a dreamily easy first week. He "went potty" without inhibition and accepted his treats with glee.

And then, inexplicably, he stopped.

He literally went from doing his business with abandon (the kind that leaves its signature on the walls at times) to shrieking in abject terror at the mention of anything bathroom related. And thus began one of the longest years of my life. That may sound dramatic, but if you too have parented a child with the ability to control his bodily functions for many days in a row, then you know what an all-consuming, stressful task convincing him to relinquish that control can be.

This was the same year that I was sourcing all the things for our first DIY house. The same year I was also nursing a baby who was only eighteen months and three days younger than his potty-averse elder brother. The same year my husband was too busy hammering and caulking and hanging drywall, in addition to meeting the responsibilities of his day job, to be around very much. The same year we rented my parents' second story after having lived as our own little family unit in our first house for three years. The same year I was trying to get my novel published. And the same year we lived away from all our friends, with whom we had zero free time to spend anyway.

During this year, I got to see my happy-go-lucky, sunny two-year-old for one, maybe two days out of the week—whichever day I had finally managed to get him to go potty. And then, as the week progressed, his personality would begin to devolve into rage and downright obstinance. I didn't like it. Nope, not one bit. It tattered my nerves and shredded my confidence as a mama. But I also understood. I mean, *I* don't feel or act great when my digestion isn't doing its thing properly, and I'm a grown woman.

I prayed (nay, *begged*) God to help my son understand that there was nothing to fear. I feverishly researched his "condition" and found solace in discovering I wasn't the only parent in the world dealing with this issue. I tried out various methods to help him get over his panic. And I spent literally hours sitting on the floor of the bathroom, keeping my boy on the potty, singing, chanting nonsense, praying, doing tricks with toy cars—*anything* to distract him long enough so that he could "go" and be himself again for a blessed day or two.

When I say that it was a hard year, it's because it took a full, complete, and entire year for us to overcome this hurdle. About six months in, I was convinced that I would still be sitting on the floor cajoling him to do his thing when he was eight. Thank the Lord this was not the case. About a week after his third birthday, following a period of gradual improvement, he suddenly decided he wasn't afraid of the potty anymore. At first, I was wary. Surely he would relapse. But he never did, praise God.

## Training Ourselves to Rely on Jesus

To say that year taught me something about training is an understatement. But it wasn't about training my child nearly as much as it was about training myself. The Lord taught me through episodes of tears and frustration, and sometimes outright clench-fisted fit throwing, that the first thing I needed to train in myself was my reliance on him.

*The Lord taught me through episodes of tears and frustration, and sometimes outright clench-fisted fit throwing, that the first thing I needed to train in myself was my reliance on him.*

Very little I did helped my son at the beginning, at least not in a tangible or obvious way. I had to keep giving him back to God each week while he grew grumpier as the days ticked by. I had to trust that this too would pass—that this would not be the defining year of my son's life (even if it sort of defined mine at the time). I had to trust that God had a purpose in this seemingly pointless ritual that chipped away at my sanity on a weekly basis.

Bit by bit, the Lord grew my prayer life (which featured near-constant references to bodily substances). He grew my patience (I once spent 70 minutes at one time camped out on the cold bathroom tile in front of the toilet). He grew my resolve (I knew I could not just let this one slide; it was my *job* as my son's mama to advocate for him in every way I could). And he grew my discipline (time management becomes very real when you have to plan certain things around your child's bathroom schedule).

Now this is certainly not the most harrowing road I have walked as a mama. But at the time, it was a necessary trial that revealed to me some areas in which I was lacking. Because you see, I have a natural bent toward child training. There's that stubborn thing I mentioned. And the fact of my own mama, who set a good example for me. And I'm pretty good with consistency in general. I don't mind repeating myself or going through the same motions *ad nauseam*. I am tenacious. As Inspector Monk would say, "It's a blessing and a curse."

I had sleep trained both my little boys from early ages. We were good at nap-time schedules. They ate what we fed them for the most part. I was decent at getting out the door on time, even with two littles and all their paraphernalia in tow. In all of that relative efficiency, it was easy to rely on my own strength instead of the Lord's. It was tempting to assume that my predisposition to training would be enough to see me through most mothering scenarios, even if I'd never encountered them before. It was confidence boosting to see my boys taking so well to my "methods."

## His Eye Is on the Sparrow

Until one of them didn't, of course. That year of potty-training purgatory humbled me in such a necessary way. But it also positively reinforced certain habits of repetition and stick-to-itiveness that have served me well over the last dozen years or so. And it ultimately taught me flexibility. (You would not *believe* what a chill potty-training mama I am these days; my older kids have literally begged me to let them potty train a sibling or two because they were ready, and I was still dragging my feet.)

But mostly, it taught me about God's goodness and his care for the seemingly insignificant (as well as monumental) worries that we face every day. If you think that he does not care about your daughter's thumb-sucking habit, think again. If I am convinced that he has abandoned me in my quest to teach my child how to read, I am mistaken. If we ever begin to doubt his care in the details, we must retrain our minds to remember this truth: "Are not two sparrows sold for a penny? Yet not one of them will fall to the ground outside your Father's care.... So don't be afraid; you are worth more than many sparrows" (Matthew 10:29-31).

But that's not all, dear, sweet, tired sisters-in-motherhood. Once we have trained our spiritual hearts to see his sovereign goodness in even the most mundane occurrences of our lives (like the time we catch sight of the book title *Everybody Poops* and dissolve into desperate, maniacal, ironic laughter), we must train our spiritual minds—armed with truth—to forge ahead into the prickliest briar patches of motherhood.

And that truth is that our children will not adhere to the narrow path when they are old unless we train them to do so. Or if they do stay on that path by the grace of God and in spite of us, it will certainly be no credit to us.

> *If we do not first choose discipline for ourselves, we cannot expect to instill such a character trait in little people whose impulse control is spotty at best and whose emotions dangle on the gossamer thread of a missed nap.*

If we do not first choose discipline for ourselves, we cannot expect to instill such a character trait in little people whose impulse control is spotty at best and whose emotions dangle on the gossamer thread of a missed nap. We must train ourselves to remember that *we*, not they, are meant to be the emotional thermostats of our own homes. And if we ever hope to keep that thermostat steady—with the pitfalls of pregnancy and postpartum hormones, sleeplessness and tyrannical three-year-olds' antics, too much to juggle and too little time in which to juggle it—we must steep our resolve in the Word of God.

A mother who does not read her Bible on a regular basis is like a ship whose rudder has been ripped from its stern. Without training ourselves to continually steer life's craft toward Scripture, we will drift in eddies of confusion or find ourselves caught in the current of cultural trends. What the Bible makes plainly evident will be muddied by a desire for ease or a quick fix.

But wait, Abbie. Didn't you just say that there's already too much to do and too little time in which to do it? How am I going to add an hour of Bible study to my day without losing my ever-loving mind?

a
mother
who does not read
her Bible on a regular basis is
like a ship whose rudder has been
ripped from its stern.

# He Gently Leads Those with Young

First, no one said anything about an hour. I think that we may automatically default to that as some sort of gold standard of holiness. But nowhere in Scripture does it mandate a specific amount of time in quiet biblical contemplation to start our day. Scripture is far from militant or prescriptive on this subject. In fact, Isaiah 40:11 says, "He tends his flock like a shepherd: He gathers the lambs in his arms and carries them close to his heart; he gently leads those that have young." I love this image of our heavenly Father caring for our babies so tenderly, but it's that last line that pulls me up short.

"He *gently* leads those that *have* young."

Wait. "Those with young"? That's *me*! Are you trying to say that the Lord *gets* it? That he cares about my overwhelm?

Yep (see above about the sparrows). Not only that, but he doesn't just leave us to wander the moors like some dumb sheep. Or drag us along with rough, impatient halter jerks. Instead, he *leads* us tenderly. And so I encourage you to ask the Lord where he would lead your Bible study.

For me, this has come to mean getting up early on the mornings that I do not already have an early fitness class to follow a Bible-in-a-year reading program and journal—in conjunction with family Bible reading led by my husband on the other days. For you, it may look entirely different. It could be ten minutes. It could be thirty. There may be candles, soft music, and color-coordinated pens. Or there may be cold coffee, a squirmy toddler, and morning breath. The important thing is to make a commitment to the Lord and then to follow his leading—to train ourselves to follow him in this discipline of prioritizing his Word.

This biblical focus is foundational to knowing how to train our children, but it's also a methodology for building meaningful consistency—not legalism—in ourselves. It is the bedrock, and without it, all other efforts will falter or fall short. It is also the most important habit we can model for our children. Honoring and valuing God's Word does not come naturally to most, me included. But once we "taste and see that the Lord is good" (Psalm 34:8), our appetite

HE *gently* LEADS THOSE THAT HAVE *young*

ISAIAH 40:11

for him only increases, and the training morphs into desiring his presence. Our children notice this and are drawn to it.

## A Biblical Gut Check

I don't know about you, but I'm all about training that happens as a natural outflow of something I'm already doing (because there's plenty of straightforward, intentional instruction that has to happen too).

I have plenty of thoughts on how to "get a two-year-old to do such and such" from a practical perspective, but ultimately, the first questions I want to ask any mama who approaches me with such a query are these:

1. Do you love and prioritize God's Word in your home?
2. Do you rely on the Lord for wisdom and direction?
3. Are you willing to be consistent and dogged in your pursuit of his goodness for you and your children?
4. Have you trained yourself to "love what must be done," as wise mama of six Ruth Chou Simons often says?

If the answer to any of the questions is a consistent no, you are not alone. Child training is hard. Self-training might be even harder, especially in a culture that daily nudges us toward a gospel of cheap grace and loving myself "just as I am" (and not in a gospel hymn sort of way either). Self-training requires a desire to "do better" as unto the Lord and see genuine, heart-stirring change. Self-training requires honest self-reflection. And self-training requires the indwelling of the Holy Spirit and a sensitivity to his leading. It is a whole lot of work. But it is worth the effort. Effort that bears so much fruit in our children's lives and our own (not to mention the lives of our husbands, friends, coworkers, and family members). Effort that stands the test of time and bequeaths its benefits to many generations to come.

It may have taken me a year to potty train my oldest child, but I have a feeling it will take a lifetime to train my heart to love Jesus more than anything else. Praise God it is a day-by-day process that we can choose to embrace, by his strength and for his glory.

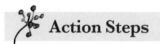 ## The Narrative

| MEDIOCRE MOTHERHOOD | CHRISTLIKE MOTHERHOOD |
| --- | --- |
| Thinks that "training" should be saved for Olympic athletes | Recognizes training as an essential part of the Christian life |
| Resents self-discipline | Pursues the fruit of the Spirit (including self-control) |
| Avoids responsibility | Embraces the fact that the buck stops (and starts) with us |

## Action Steps

- Memorize and meditate on 2 Timothy 3:16 (ESV): "All Scripture is breathed out by God and profitable for teaching, for reproof, for correction, and for training in righteousness."

- Identify three areas in which you lack discipline; choose one to focus on this week.

- Make a plan to incorporate regular Scripture reading (we love *The One Year Bible*) and memorization into your routine.

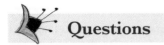 **Questions**

How can I be more consistent to do the "needful things" that draw me close to God and help my household run more smoothly?

Am I disciplined in some areas but lack fortitude when it comes to studying God's Word? Why?

If I am facing overwhelm, how much of that is a result of my own lack of self-training?

 **Prayer**

*Lord, you gave us the perfect example of discipline in Jesus, who was "obedient to death—even death on a cross" (Philippians 2:8). May we emulate his example, knowing that whatever discomfort we experience in the self-training process will ultimately produce great fruit.*

# The Gentleness Challenge

## PRACTICAL HOPE FOR ANGRY MOMS

Three weeks before I gave birth to my identical twin boys, Titus and Tobias, our beagle, Ruby, gave birth to multiples of her own—six adorable puppies. During my last painful weeks of pregnancy, I watched her navigate her first painful weeks of motherhood. And I saw some humorous parallels to many of my own experiences (observing her nursing multiple puppies at once definitely gave me flashbacks to tandem feeding Evy and Nola).

But never did I feel more connected with Ruby than I did the night she went missing. Her pups were only four weeks old and still nursing heavily, but one night, after we celebrated my birthday with family at our house, Ruby was nowhere to be found. She was such a good mama dog that we had a hard time believing she had abandoned her babies, which immediately raised questions of what evil fate might have befallen her.

The kids remembered hearing her howling near the edge of the woods, and my mind hopscotched from one image to the next of Ruby's last brave stand against a coyote or a rabid raccoon. We checked every closet and the garage. We combed our property with flashlights. We hopped in the truck to troll the dark roads. No Ruby.

Feeling sick, I begged God to bring her back. I'm not much of a dog person, but I love our Ruby-girl. Not only that, but her babies needed their mama. I tried to picture dropper feeding puppies in addition to nursing newborn twins, and my stomach churned at the prospect.

Then, just when my hope began to wane, I received a message from my mom: "Ruby's with us. Apparently, she jumped in the back with the leftover food from your birthday, and your dad didn't notice her when he shut the trunk. She spent the whole ride to our house chowing down."

You guys, Ruby hadn't faced off against a bobcat and lost. She'd had herself a little mama-cation in the back of my parents' Honda Civic—huddling quietly in the dark as she stuffed her face.

How many postpartum nursing mamas can relate? That dog wasn't lost. She was *hangry*!

## Hormones Are Real, but They Don't Tell the Truth

I remember feeling like I would give anything to eat my feelings in a dark, quiet room after I had our eighth baby. My hormones were so out of whack, and my fuse was short.

I wouldn't say that patience is naturally my strongest suit, but it is something the Lord has been gracious to grow throughout my mothering career, so by the time I had Shiloh, many of the quirks and nuisances that would have genuinely annoyed me in the past were mere blips of frustration or even amusement. Or at least they had been with number three and even number six. But not so after number eight.

*If hormones are anything,
they are easily offended.*

I'd suffered from moderate postpartum depression after Evy and Nola's birth. But this was different. Every one of my senses was heightened in the most uncomfortable way, and my offendometer was set to "high." If hormones are anything, they are easily offended. And rightfully so. Because clearly your seven-year-old is purposefully smacking his lips while he chews, and the toddler peed in his pants because he wants the last thread of your sanity to snap.

Some days, I woke up mad and went to bed in a huff. In between, I gave my grumpy self too much grace. I'd love to say that my kids didn't notice, but the truth is that my oldest had just reached the age of noticing everything (and often blowing it out of proportion, which made two of us).

I know there are many mamas reading this right now who can relate and others who are itching to fire off an email telling me to have my thyroid checked or to look into certain supplements. I get it. Looking back, I'm sure there were practical things I should have been doing, but I was too deeply in survival mode to research the right essential oils or diet changes. Just like with Ruby, being "hangry" was a very real thing with me. I would be rocking along with homeschooling, taking things in stride (because I wasn't always a grouch), and then my blood sugar would drop, and my head would suddenly feel as if a swarm of bees had taken up residence. With my buzzing brain and my grumbling stomach, there simply weren't enough functioning compensatory organs to make sense of algebra, and I'd find myself irritated at not only "y = mx + b" but also the child who'd subjected me to such an equation in the midst of a hunger crisis. There were times that Shaun would walk into a room, take one look at me, and head to the pantry for a Lärabar.

I say this to acknowledge that there were some very real physiological and psychological aspects to my struggle. But regardless of the legitimate explanations I could offer, these were the facts: Sometimes, I wasn't very nice. I knew it. My husband knew it. And my children knew it.

And something needed to be done about it.

## Something Needed to Change

Everything came to a head about two months postpartum when I descended the stairs to discover much the same scene as before I'd lain down for a Sunday nap. We don't do much cleaning on Sundays, but we were hosting a church small group at the time, and there were always messes to clean up before "company" came over. I had my list, and the kids had theirs. But unfortunately, they'd done a less-than-stellar job of completing their tasks.

*Their carelessness felt personal, which is something I've since come to recognize as a symptom of hormonal overwhelm.*

Their carelessness felt personal, which is something I've since come to recognize as a symptom of hormonal overwhelm. My emotions were telling me that my kids didn't respect or love me, that they had purposefully left that toy on the ground, even while my seasoned Mom Brain assured me that no, kids are just capable of walking right by a mess without even noticing it and will often do the bare minimum if you're not standing by to help them choose diligence.

I couldn't seem to reconcile the two conflicting narratives. So I lectured. I didn't yell or rant (okay, there was some ranting). But I did harp. It was not my finest motherhood moment.

And all the while, I felt the small, insistent voice of the Holy Spirit whispering, "It doesn't have to be like this."

*In ten years, will **any** of the temporary stress relief you get from fussing about something that seems like a big deal **now** have been worth the lasting effect of your harsh words about it on your children?*

Later that evening, after our small group had gone home, Shaun sat me down and very kindly told me that while he understood my frustration, I couldn't let it consume me. He was calm about it, but his words reverberated in my soul like the clanging of a morning wake-up bell. I spent some time in prayer and self-reflection afterward, and this was the thought that clarified, bright and sharp, in my mind and heart: In ten years, will *any* of the temporary stress relief you get from fussing about something that seems like a big deal *now* have been worth the lasting effect of your harsh words about it on your children?

I knew the answer: a thousand times no.

## Hormones Don't Excuse Sin

I thought about how I wanted the kids to remember me: loving, patient, even-tempered, fun, resourceful, always willing to help. I knew that I had been many of these things through the years, and I was trusting that two months of struggle would not define my children's recollections of me. But I couldn't in good conscience, as a Christian mother, keep shoving aside the conviction that hormones or no hormones, my reactions were sinful.

*I couldn't in good conscience, as a Christian mother, keep shoving aside the conviction that hormones or no hormones, my reactions were sinful.*

This acknowledgment is unpopular in the realm of secular motherhood. And I understand why. It stings. And it requires action. The culture of mediocre motherhood focuses on wallowing in the hard and celebrating our shortcomings as proof that we are all human and "in this together." I remember one mother's response to a post I wrote about the fact that motherhood had not lessened me: "Good for you," she said. "But some of us are just over here fighting to get the word out that motherhood has utterly wrecked us, and we are not okay. We are working so hard to have our voices heard and our feelings legitimized."

As much as I believe that motherhood does, indeed, wreck all of us in one way or another, I know that from a biblical perspective, simply "getting the word out" so that we can all indulge in a huddle of motherhood misery is not the answer. Honoring the hard is important. But we can't stay there. Focusing on the struggle only leads to bitterness and a feeling of having been cheated. "I didn't sign up for this. The Hallmark cards lied to me with their photoshopped images of shiny-haired, happy mothers and smudge-free children."

I agree. That's not honest motherhood. But neither is saying, "*Since* I feel duped, I'm entitled to dwell in my disappointment for the rest of eternity."

It's not fair to our children. It's not fair to our husbands. It's not fair to ourselves. And it's an affront to the freedom for which Christ has set us free (Galatians 5:1). Because Christianity is radical in its approach to being "not okay." Instead of encouraging us to seek out others who are similarly "wrecked" for comfort, Jesus says, "Come to me, all you who are weary and heavy laden, and I will give you rest" (Matthew 11:28).

I'm tempted to heave a hefty sigh of relief at those words, but then I read the second half: "Take my yoke upon you and learn from me, for I am gentle and humble in heart, and you will find rest for your souls. For my yoke is easy and my burden is light" (Matthew 11:29-30). The words "yoke" and "burden" hardly sound restful. But that is the beautiful paradox of following Christ. In taking up his mantle of humility and gentleness, we lay down the right to cling to our overwhelm and the desire to have our struggles affirmed by our peers. And once we've pried our fingers off of those entitled feelings and fixed our eyes on Jesus, we find that his burden is, indeed, light and freeing.

## A Is for Accountability

Of course, godly accountability bears little resemblance to a cycle of complaining and commiseration. And I found myself wanting to create a community of like-minded women who could encourage and uplift each other in the pursuit of dulling our razor blade tongues.

And so I started the Gentleness Challenge, an Instagram account that focused on using only kind speech and calm tones for thirty days. We weren't allowed to gripe at anyone or about anyone. We could acknowledge our struggles but only with the goal of praying for and holding each other accountable.

In taking up CHRIST'S mantle of humility and gentleness, we lay down the right to cling to our overwhelm and the desire to have our struggles affirmed by our peers.

Thousands of women joined immediately, and my suspicion that I couldn't possibly be alone in grappling with my erratic post-baby hormones was confirmed as woman after woman described her desire to address her family with gentleness and a happy spirit—a desire that often warred with the yelling and nagging that were actually dominating the tone of their homes.

It's so easy to become convinced that our current struggles must define our future circumstances as well. We wake up with the same frustration for a week or two months or even a year, and it starts to feel like our "new normal." And all the while, we know that "if God is for us" (and he is), then "who can be against us?" (Romans 8:31). Also, "he who is in you is greater than he who is in the world" (1 John 4:4 ESV). And again, "his divine power has given us everything we need for a godly life" (2 Peter 1:3).

I already believed each of these verses before I had Shiloh, but it's alarming how quickly convictions can get snowed under by feelings, which is why I will never launch a campaign to have my feelings legitimized. They're too fickle, too liable to rise and fall with the ocean swell of my circumstances. But a movement to submit my feelings to the lordship of Jesus Christ? *That* I can get behind!

So after my conversation with Shaun and then the Lord, I gathered my children and apologized for being a sourpuss. And I embarked on thirty days of nothing but gentle speech.

## Anger Detox

I would expect each of you to point a bold finger at me—à la the old hag in *The Princess Bride*—and cry, "Liar!" if I were to claim that the challenge was easy. James 3:8 says, "No human being can tame the tongue. It is a restless evil, full of deadly poison." Youch. That sounds hopeless, right? But notice it says that no *human* can tame the tongue. And yet in Matthew 19:26 Jesus said, "With man this is impossible, but with God all things are possible." (He wasn't specifically talking about reining in our speech, but the principle still applies.)

I discovered the depth of truth in Jesus's words as I woke up each day and submitted my words and my attitude to God. I also shared what he was teaching me with the other women in the challenge and learned from them as well.

Within three days, much of the angst that had been plaguing my thoughts began to wane. The jittery, anxious feelings and the hair-trigger anger began to subside as well. The more I shoveled my feelings in the Lord's direction, instead of at my family, the less important my feelings, well, *felt*—in the best possible way.

I began to recognize myself again, not because "myself" had done a perfect job of speaking gently before but because my previous ungodly tendencies had felt so amplified for the previous several months that it felt as if a different person—a rage monster—had taken up residence in my brain and body.

The first week felt almost like a detox from something addictive—akin to the times I have done a sugar fast. My blood sugar would plummet as I was coming in the door in the late afternoon, arms loaded with groceries, surrounded by famished children who all wanted to know what was for dinner (and took turns asking the dreaded question one after the other, only to loop back around to declare, "I forgot. What's for dinner again?" just to make it extra fun). My pulse would begin to pound in rhythm with my aching head, and the words "For the love of Pete, would you just! be! quiet!" would percolate right behind my lips.

Honestly, I don't think anyone—not even Pete—would have blamed me. But I had made a promise to use only gentle speech for 30 days, and taking Pete's name in vain did not qualify. Sometimes, the best I could do was start with a strong "*Guys!*" and then tone it down to a milder "Mama's head hurts, and she needs to get dinner started. Please quiet down." Other times, I didn't say anything—just dropped the armload of groceries and headed for the porch to breathe. When all else failed, I *literally* bit my tongue.

It was a process. But minute by minute, hour by hour, day by day, the Lord grew my resolve and renewed my mind and with it my speech. And I learned something: Even though my hormones were very real, and it would be easy to assume that nothing I was practicing *should* have had any effect on my body's chemistry, as the month progressed, I was experiencing clearer thoughts, fewer episodes of "bees in my brain," and less "hanger."

Could it be that using the excuse of my wonky hormones to indulge my impatience had actually made my symptoms worse? Proverbs 16:24 (ESV) says,

GRACIOUS WORDS ARE LIKE A HONEYCOMB

PROVERBS 16:24 ESV

"Gracious words are like a honeycomb, sweetness to the soul and health to the body." It stands to reason, then, that ungracious words can produce an adverse effect on our well-being. Allowing myself to express my frustrations had enabled my hormones to rage unchecked in my system. But when I made certain words and tones off limits, I began retraining the neural pathways of my brain toward gratitude and positivity—a process that Scripture calls the "renewing of your mind" (Romans 12:2) and one that secular science is finding more and more support for. I find it fascinating how the Lord has created us as holistic beings. The physical affects the emotional, which can bolster or wreak havoc on the spiritual.

## A Gentleness Game Plan

I emerged from the first Gentleness Challenge a changed woman. I'm not prone to hair-trigger emotions, and I've long held a goal of speaking to everyone with civility, as to the Lord. But I had never focused specifically on gentleness. And once I did, I recognized an area that needed more help than I'd been willing to acknowledge before—especially in light of how much the Bible has to say on the subject.

Colossians 3:12 says, "As God's chosen people, holy and dearly loved, clothe yourselves with compassion, kindness, humility, gentleness and patience."

Ephesians 4:2 admonishes us to "be completely humble and gentle; be patient, bearing with one another in love."

And of course, the famous "fruit of the Spirit" in Galatians 5:22-23 includes gentleness with love, joy, peace, self-control, and other stellar attributes.

The more I memorized verses on gentleness, read about it, and focused on using only gentle speech, the more the Lord showed me just how key this concept is to motherhood. And the more of a habit it became.

I've hosted the challenge multiple times since that first one, and the Lord has been faithful to reveal something new to me each time. But the "steps for success" that have made the most impact on me (and others who have shared their experiences) are these.

*1. Acknowledge the problem without making excuses.* I know this sounds like the beginning of an AA meeting, but as I mentioned before, negativity has an addictive quality, and until we call it what it is without trying to pass it off as something nicer, we can't begin the process of claiming freedom from our enslavement to it.

*2. Repent of unkindness and reject it completely.* I've heard of people with generally clean speech giving themselves permission to use whatever curse words they want on Saturdays—a sort of "language cheat day." Not only am I dubious about the biblical logic behind such a practice, since Scripture exhorts us to let "no unwholesome talk come out of [our] mouths" (Ephesians 4:29 BSB), but I also know from experience that this concept would fail miserably in the realm of gentle speech. I was able to improve in this area only by consistently and tenaciously clinging by the grace of God to my resolve to use exclusively kind speech. Only a resolve to utterly forsake complaining and criticizing effected real change. (Notice I did *not* say perfection.)

*3. Tell somebody about your goal.* Obviously, I went a little big with this one, since I invited all my online friends to participate. But even more impactful (and scarier) was the decision to tell my kids what I was doing. If you've ever been taken to task by a six-year-old who objects to your not following the *exact* errand schedule you casually threw out in the car that morning, then you know that despite their complete inability to keep track of their own shoes, small children are tenacious accountability partners for the things that matter to them. After telling my kids about the Gentleness Challenge, I invited them to join me, and they did! We rewarded especially kind speech with pennies from our Penny Reward System (more on that soon) and removed pennies for rude or harsh words—a habit that has stuck to this day.

*4. Memorize Scripture.* During the Gentleness Challenge, the kids and I memorized all of Ephesians 4, which has so many good reminders about how we treat others and was an excellent source of encouragement to all of us as the month progressed.

*5. Pray.* This one may sound cliché, but it's absolutely key, especially when we have a tendency to try to use our own strength alone to plow through any barriers we encounter. The Gentleness Challenge helped me become proficient in what I call "bullet prayers" ("Jesus, give me kind speech," "Lord, help me be calm," "Father, show me how to be gentle"), which allowed me to pause for a beat and swallow the sharp phrase that was just itching to fly out of my mouth.

I started out this chapter with a zany story about my dog, Ruby, and her coping mechanisms when she was overcome by hunger and being needed constantly. And I'm ending it with a reminder that we are much more complicated beings than those of the canine persuasion. As much as we might feel like a nice quiet drive with snacks is the cure for what ails us (and as much as we might be right to some extent), the reality is that the Lord often takes our struggles and uses them as tools to show us just how desperately we need his strength and grace each day. Birthday leftovers are good. But Jesus is always better.

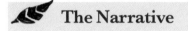 ## The Narrative

| MEDIOCRE MOTHERHOOD | CHRISTLIKE MOTHERHOOD |
|---|---|
| Resents the suggestion that hormones do not excuse a multitude of sins | Knows that only Christ's love covers a multitude of sins |
| Focuses on grace to the exclusion of personal responsibility | Refuses to use grace as an excuse not to grow |
| Feels shamed by admonishments to "do better" | Feels empowered by knowing that in Christ, we can choose gentle speech |

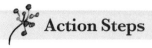 **Action Steps**

- Memorize and meditate on Ephesians 4:2 (ESV): "Be completely humble and gentle; be patient, bearing with one another in love."
- Sit down and identify symptoms of hormonal overwhelm.
- Outline three practical steps (such as the Gentleness Challenge, eating snacks regularly, taking fifteen-minute power naps, or unfollowing off-base social media accounts) to overcome the urges to take out bad days on your family.

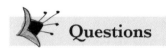 **Questions**

In what ways am I "completely humble and gentle"? In what ways am I not?

If I were to ask my kids to describe my speech, what would they say?

How can I invite my whole family into my efforts to use gentle speech?

**Prayer**

*Lord, you are so patient with us, slow to anger and abounding in love (Numbers 14:18). Teach us to follow your example and check our rough, impatient speech at the door of our mouths.*

# Training Our Kids in the Way They Should Go

## FOUR PRINCIPLES FOR INSTILLING GOOD HABITS

In the last two chapters, we talked about practical ways to train ourselves—ways to deepen our love for God's Word, to discipline our minds and bodies to do the hard things (whether we feel like it or not), to pursue gentle speech, and to be consistent in turning to the Lord for strength and help—which are *all good* things! (I would definitely be inserting all the hand-clapping emojis if this were a social media post.)

But what do those methods of shaping our own character have to do practically with a thirteen-month-old who wakes up four times a night? Or a mouthy five-year-old? Or a whiny two-year-old? Or an angsty fifteen-year-old?

A lot, actually.

And how does biblical child training differ from the worldly perspective of child-rearing—one that leads, all too often, down the path of mediocre motherhood?

A lot, actually.

# Elite Athletes Do It. We Should Too.

You see, "training" is often viewed as a dirty word in secular parenting circles. I've even seen it called "ugly." After all, our children are not dogs. They are human beings with complex needs and emotions and nuances. I've often heard those who oppose the idea of training children say things such as "I'm not teaching my children so much as learning from them," and "Let your children be your guide." These phrases sound very earthy and wise but quickly show their lack of substance when pitted against even the mildest toddler meltdown. I'm not exactly sure what I'm supposed to learn from my two-year-old's tendency to throw himself down on the filthy grocery store floor and comingle his hot tears with the gum from someone's shoe, other than that he is a sinner and—based on how irritated I can get at this behavior—so am I. But I certainly hope that I am teaching him something about how we respond to our sinful tendencies.

Because while I agree that (a) kids are complex emotional and spiritual beings for whom training should look very different than for animals and (b) we can learn much from their better qualities, I would be lying if I said that I didn't genuinely believe an abdication of our roles of training our children is also an abdication of excellence in motherhood. Just like an Olympic gymnast would never forgo a rigorous training course if she wants to win the gold, we would be shortsighted as parents to choose the seemingly easy road of passive parenting if we desire to "press on toward the goal to win the prize for which God has called (us) heavenward in Christ Jesus" (Philippians 3:14). Because what appears to be the easier choice in the short term eventually reveals itself as very difficult, indeed, when we encounter significant behavioral and relational snarls in the future. Not only that, but the Bible asks more of us, which is why it is so key to first invest in training ourselves.

If we have not first trained ourselves to persevere through the hard when necessary, how can we expect our children to face with any level of equanimity their "crumbly" clothes (my four-year-old's panicky description of any article of clothing with wrinkles—which, as a mama with a rather full schedule that did not include much ironing, was all of them)? If we have not first modeled dependence upon Christ day in and day out, how can we encourage our kids to turn to Jesus in their times of need? If we have not read our Bibles, how can we even know what Scripture has to say about our responsibilities to our own off-spring, much less imagine that they will want to find out more for themselves?

Don't get me wrong: We are not Jesus. We cannot save our children, nor can we vouch for their righteousness. We cannot convict them at a heart level. Only the Holy Spirit can do that. Not only that, but any secular parent who wants "results" more than holiness could, with enough effort, produce well-trained children.

*We can lay a foundation of righteousness that will hold them in good stead as they grow and mature and (God willing) develop a relationship with the Lord that is all their own.*

What we can do is lay a foundation of righteousness that will hold them in good stead as they grow and mature and (God willing) develop a relationship with the Lord that is all their own. And one of the main ways we can do that is by teaching them to "act justly and to love mercy and to walk humbly" (Micah 6:8) while under our roofs.

## We Mamas Are Truth-Tellers

Have you ever seen a two-year-old's version of justice? It goes something like this: Two-year-old steals his baby brother's belongings. He's not picky; anything will do. The two-year-old is happy and fulfilled, despite the fact that his eight-month-old brother is wailing inconsolably because his paci has been snatched from his mouth and is now being swung around his older brother's head by the tether like a lasso as he wanders around the room placidly ignoring his brother's misery. Life is good, and there is no wrong in the world. At least for the two-year-old.

Two minutes later, the two-year-old's five-year-old sister saunters into the room and grabs the paci-lasso away from the thief, returning it to her baby brother and then casually swiping the two-year-old's favorite toy truck out of his hands as she turns to leave. The two-year-old explodes with impotent rage. How *dare* someone older and bigger than he prey on his innocence in such a depraved and calloused manner? There is weeping and gnashing of teeth. There will be blood (but really, there might be if that teeth gnashing turns into ear biting).

The two-year-old makes *zero* connection between his sister's nefarious conduct and his own clearly innocent and completely justifiable treatment of his baby brother. Why? Because he is a sinner. Which means that he's a selfish little navel-gazer (a few of you just gasped). A *cute* little navel-gazer, capable of the best hugs and the sweetest moments of darling behavior, I grant you—but a navel-gazer nonetheless.

 *Regardless of our personalities—whether bold and confrontational or peace-loving and mild—we mamas are truth-tellers.*

And his version of "justice" is always going to be skewed in his favor. It's how we're wired as sinners, little or big. Which means that it's our job as mamas to preach truth, not only to ourselves but to our two-year-olds, our twenty-six-year-olds, and every age in between (and beyond). Regardless of our personalities—whether bold and confrontational or peace-loving and mild—we mamas are truth-tellers. We must be. Or we have failed to fulfill one of the primary biblical mandates about God's laws that we are given in Deuteronomy 6:7 (BSB): "You shall teach them diligently to your children and speak of them when you sit at home and when you walk along the road, when you lie down and when you get up."

YOU
SHALL TEACH
THEM
DILIGENTLY
TO
YOUR CHILDREN

DEUTERONOMY 6:7 BSB

It's a whole thing.

It's why I have hammered so strongly our need to not only know *of* God's Word but to internalize it in a way that makes it come alive for our children in a variety of circumstances.

## Great, but How Do I Do That?

Confession: When I read this part of this chapter to my husband, he said, "I like it! But I have a feeling most Christian women will read it and think, 'Yes, this! But what does that look like practically speaking?'"

I have that same feeling every time anyone answers a very pragmatic question of mine with a seemingly theoretical answer. Yes, that's nice. But could you be more specific?

I can. And I will. Promise. But I want to first convey something foundational here, which I will attempt to do with a rather hackneyed old proverb you may have heard once or twice before: "Give a man a fish, and you feed him for a day. Teach a man to fish, and you feed him for a lifetime."

This is my goal. Because chances are, I've encountered enough antics from two-year-olds that I can help you out at least a little with whatever quandary you bring me from your two-year-old.

Teething? I can help with that.

Potty training? Check.

Whining? That too.

But my question for you first is this: Do you simply want your toddler to stop (whatever) *now* so that you get temporary relief and a return to sanity? Or do you want to begin instilling biblical precepts in him that will help him to desire righteousness and a genuine relationship with the Lord in the future?

The two are hardly mutually exclusive, and I am going to balk at anyone's suggestion that simply speaking to the heart of the matter will be enough to produce consistent, lasting behavioral change.

Because actions are so, so important. In fact, many times, if we aren't training the behavior, we won't be able to reach our children's hearts in order to plant those deep seeds of truth (because a six-year-old who doesn't know how to listen may never internalize any of the biblical goodness we impart during family devotionals). We're training our children to love righteousness, justice, and mercy by modeling for them what those look like practically (which is why we require the two-year-old to give the paci back and the five-year-old to apologize for taking the toy truck).

Jesus didn't just tell his disciples to meditate on his death and suffering in order to commemorate his sacrifice on the cross. He didn't exhort them to feel it in their hearts. Instead, he gave them specific action steps: *Drink this cup and eat this bread in remembrance of me.* Why? "For whenever you eat this bread and drink this cup, you proclaim the Lord's death until he comes" (1 Corinthians 11:26).

If we simply memorize verses with our children but never put them into practice because we trust that the rote retention of Scripture will be enough to produce obedience and kindness, we will be sorely disappointed when we realize that our ten-year-old can spout the fruits of the Spirit chapter and verse but doesn't have enough self-control to keep from saying every typically preteen thing that pops into her head.

It's just like James 1:22-24 says: "Do not merely listen to the word, and so deceive yourselves. Do what it says. Anyone who listens to the word but does not do what it says is like someone who looks at his face in a mirror and, after looking at himself, goes away and immediately forgets what he looks like."

Yes, the Word has the power to transform, but only if we obey what it says.

Of course, we also miss the mark if we train our children to speak politely for the sake of "being nice." As I mentioned above, training does not have to be an exclusively scriptural parenting approach. My dad used to tell me stories of how his own mother, who was a staunch unbeliever, trained her five boys to behave perfectly in public and then allowed them to run amok at home. She cared more about people's *perception* of her children's goodness than the goodness itself.

In Matthew 12:34 (esv), Jesus says, "For out of the abundance of the heart the mouth speaks." In other words, we can whitewash our words with winsomeness, but at a certain point, what we really think *will* come out. With kids, that point is usually earlier rather than later. (Honor's propensity for referring to my pregnant belly as "hugenormous" when I was pregnant with our second set of twins is proof of that.) Only if we have been diligent to bury the goodness of God's Word deep in our children's souls and practice it on a daily basis will we have done our part to ensure that what springs up inside them and issues forth from their mouths is a reflection of God's truth.

## No One Has Kids Because They're Easy

Years ago, at vacation Bible school, someone told me, "I would totally have more kids if mine were as well-behaved as yours."

The comment took me aback, partly because I had just caught my two-year-old swiping cookies off the dessert table right after I talked my four-year-old twin girls down from yet another precipice of emotional catastrophe. (If you already thought four-year-old emotions were loud, I can assure you that they're deafening in stereo.) My kids are sweet and capable of great kindness, but they're also just that: kids. They are well-equipped to drive me and each other bonkers with their propensity for leaving socks in random corners, intentionally and loudly singing the wrong lyrics on repeat to get a rise out of siblings, dumping grape juice on the living room rug, and beating each other over the head with foam swords.

I was also a bit bemused by the suggestion that we had continued to have children because of their angelic natures. This woman was a Christian—and a staunch Calvinist at that. She knew that theologically speaking, there was no way I had produced six (at the time) naturally obedient offspring. And she *should* have known that even if one child happens to be compliant, that is certainly no guarantee that any future siblings will have equally mild and malleable temperaments.

No.

Their helpfulness and pliancy—when manifested—were a result of years of invested prayer, discipline, and training. I don't say this to imply that I can produce true goodness in my children. As 1 Corinthians 3:6-8 says,

I planted the seed, Apollos watered it, but God has been making it grow. So neither the one who plants nor the one who waters is anything, but only God, who makes things grow. The one who plants and the one who waters have one purpose, and they will each be rewarded according to their own labor.

I truly believe that my greatest and holiest purpose as a mother is to point my children to Jesus—to *train* them in his ways. But I cannot claim any credit for any success in *keeping* them in his ways. That is God's doing.

## Four Core Principles of Child Training

Still, I genuinely believe that certain universal principles of child training can be applied to just about any situation that involves children. And I have become more convinced of these principles the longer I've been a mother and the more children I've had, even *though* each child has displayed distinct preferences and a unique personality pretty much from the moment of birth.

The core values of child training that my husband and I adhere to, no matter the personality or the scenario, are these:

communication

consistency

discipline

follow-through

It sounds so basic in principle. But, my, how hard it can be in practice! By the time Evy and Nola came along, I had already taught three children how to read, use the potty, buckle their own car seats, and eat with utensils. Before the "twinsies" ever reached the "terrible twos" (which is a misnomer in my opinion; I'll take a two-year-old over a threenager any old day), I was fairly well versed in young children's milestones and felt reasonably convinced our four training foundations were key components in surviving some of the more difficult stages that I had encountered.

Truth be told, in many ways the twinsies were *easier* as babies than singletons. They slept all night from an early age, snuggled head to head. They kept each other entertained. They seemed to compete for cuteness at certain points. They were so much fun!

But then they reached the age of two years and nine months, and most—I won't say all—of that changed. They became moody, even histrionic, over seemingly insignificant things, like a butter knife that had—gasp—butter on it (no, I didn't make that up). They voiced their big emotions in tones and decibel levels that left our ears ringing. (At least the ringing in our ears dulled the screaming a bit.) And they began to despise their car seats, which made our daily hour-long round-trip drives to the gym where I taught classes a misery. I genuinely wondered if Theo, whose infant car seat sat between theirs, would suffer hearing loss.

The kicker? They changed clothes 18,972 times a day. Okay, fine, it was only eight. But I'm not exaggerating that number. Before we nipped that particular little quirk in the bud, I felt like most of the moments I wasn't homeschooling, cleaning up spills, breastfeeding, reading stories, and making food, I spent picking up articles of clothing from every dang corner of the house. It was a full-time job that I did not want, need, or apply for (other than the whole birthing of the children who "employed" me, I suppose). And it was entirely up to me to quit it (the clothes retrieval, not the mothering).

So what did I do? I applied my tried-and-true methods of communication, consistency, discipline, and follow-through in very practical ways.

## Practical Ways to Teach Your Kids to "Be a Blessing"

First, I communicated the behavior I expected from my girls. This is *huge* and yet so basic that we often forget this step and simply throw everybody in the car willy-nilly to run errands. When we tumble out at the grocery store with no briefing or plan, we wonder why everyone seems intent on touching at least three surfaces of every item in the store. The answer? They weren't reminded about protocol. Whenever anyone asks me how in the world I am able to run errands with multiple children without feeling (too) frazzled, I tell them that a huge part of this is conveying my expectations to said children before we ever get out of our giant bus.

To the best of my ability, I let them know how many stops we need to make, about how long we're going to be gone in terms the smallest children can understand (not "two hours" but "back by lunchtime"), and what I need from them (oldest to hold the youngest's hand, middle to grab a grocery cart, everyone to keep their hands to themselves unless asked to help grab something).

And I always remind them that wherever we go and whatever we do, we want to "be a blessing"—our family motto.

It doesn't mean they always do exactly what I ask—not by a long shot—but at least they are equipped with what they *should* be doing in any given scenario, which sets us up for success instead of confusion.

In the case of the twinsies' clothes-swapping obsession, communication meant I told them that once they were dressed, they were to wear those clothes until either they were too soiled to wear anymore or we changed into pajamas. If they didn't follow my instructions, there would be consequences. And I consistently conveyed this each day (necessary because they were so young).

When it came to discipline, it had a twofold meaning:

1. It required discipline on my part to be consistent with communicating my expectations.

2. I had to be willing to offer appropriate discipline when the twins didn't obey the guidelines that I'd clearly given them.

Last, but so far from least, I had to follow through—and do so right away. For me, that meant applying consequences, such as early bedtimes and lost privileges, and the painstaking job of following two two-year-olds through the house as they picked up and "folded" (ever seen a toddler fold an article of clothing?) all their discarded clothes, took them to their room, and replaced them in drawers.

Too often, timely follow-through is the point of training at which our will fails. We might consistently tell our children what we expect of them and discuss discipline, but when it comes to actually doing what we say we're going to do, we peter out. Why? Because follow-through is often even more inconvenient for us than for our children. (Ever used the phrase "It would be so much easier just to do it myself?" Yeah, me too.) Especially the kind of follow-through that requires us to immediately stop whatever important thing we're currently doing and to fully engage with the situation at hand.

For the girls' daily dress-up binges, follow-through looked like locking their bedroom door, the most practical of training strategies (limiting access). This step was as much a punishment for me as for them, since their room was on the second floor and they shared it with Della, who relied on me to unlock the door each time she needed something from her room. It also meant that the girls no longer spent much time playing happily in their room.

I dedicated more time dealing with this issue than when I had done all the picking up myself. Even if I didn't love retrieving crumpled shorts and tops from every corner of my house, I could still do it a whole heap of a lot faster than my girls. And every time I sent them to bed early for cramming in three rapid-fire changes of clothes right before pajamas while I nursed their brother, I was met with wails of despair and rage. It would have been so much easier to let it slide and hope they had forgotten the promised consequences.

## Mirroring God's Faithful Character to Our Kids

I can almost hear you saying, "But what about grace, Abbie? Do we always have to do exactly what we say?" Not necessarily. We are allowed to change gears halfway through the day. And grace is important. We have multiple opportunities to offer our children the grace of a less-strict-than-promised response every single day. And we can teach powerful truths about God's grace-filled approach

We have been entrusted
with the privilege of
"training our children in
the way they should go"
as a reflection of the
care, effort, & love
that God invests
in us.

to us when we choose those opportunities wisely. But if we make "letting it slide" the rule rather than the exception, we communicate something worrisome to our children, something that undoes a great deal of any other consistency or discipline that we have worked so hard to establish: the idea that we do not really mean what we say. And when we do not follow through on our promises (whether those of discipline or reward), we inadvertently communicate to our children that their heavenly Father won't honor his either.

Because that is the ultimate truth about training: We have been entrusted with the privilege of "training our children in the way they should go" as a reflection of the care, effort, and love that God invests in us. To give in when it is hard or inconvenient is an inaccurate portrayal of our Father God's commitment to our holiness. Yes, we will lack steadfastness at times. But he never does. And the more we train *ourselves* to prioritize consistency and follow-through, the better we mirror his faithful character for our children.

## The Narrative

| MEDIOCRE MOTHERHOOD | CHRISTLIKE MOTHERHOOD |
| --- | --- |
| Adopts a "child-led" approach | Accepts the role of parent and leader |
| Dreads the repetition of training | Chooses consistency as an act of worship |
| Avoids follow-through when it's unpleasant or inconvenient | Follows through, even when it's hard |

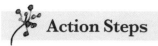

## Action Steps

- Memorize and meditate on Hebrews 12:11 (ESV): "For the moment all discipline seems painful rather than pleasant, but later it yields the peaceful fruit of righteousness to those who have been trained by it."

- Choose three things that will help you practically with staying consistent in training your kids. (My favorites are alarms as reminders to do something, timers to stay on track, and simple prep like laying out shoes and snacks before leaving the house.)

- Place scriptural affirmations of the benefits of training around your home as motivation to keep going.

## Questions

In what ways am I embracing my God-given position as "mama" rather than "best bud?" In what ways am I not?

What keeps me from being consistent or following through? How can I tweak those things?

Do I truly believe that training up my children in the way they should go will make a significant difference in their lives? If so, how am I exemplifying that?

## Prayer

*Lord, you never give up on us, no matter how stubborn or intractable we are. And we know you love us because you discipline us (Hebrews 12:6). Help us to follow your example by loving our children well enough to train them in your ways.*

# The Penny Reward System

## A SIMPLE WAY TO ENCOURAGE
## GOOD CHOICES

You might imagine that as a mama of ten who doesn't enjoy chaos, I am the queen of charts and systems. But I'm not. I despise sticker charts—not because they are so inherently despicable but because I am so inherently rubbish at, ahem, *sticking* with them. And don't get me started on felt balls for behavior, colored beads for grades, and gold stars for chores. I think the phrase "I can't even" was coined right after someone super organized excitedly explained her felt ball/bead/gold star system to someone like me, and someone like me just about died. Again, I have no objection to it as a concept. And mad props to anyone who can actually pull it off. But I know my limits, and they clearly do not extend past a single-item reward system.

I'm more of a rhythm girl than a strict scheduler. I am a fan of an uncomplicated, repetitive approach to most tasks that makes it simple for the kids and me to remember what to do without a lot of props or extra fluff—a methodology that usually serves us well. But I also tend to grit my teeth and plow through parenting obstacles without taking the time to pause and assess what practical steps might alleviate some pressure. It's helpful when we're facing a deadline or an especially challenging season. But it doesn't work as well for recurring behavioral pitfalls.

Thankfully, I have a husband who has a knack for evaluating a problematic scenario and then positing a "recipe" for a workable solution with the key ingredients being "simplicity and repetition."

## A System for Those Who "Can't Even"

Years ago, when our oldest was only ten and we were neck-deep in finishing our second DIY house build, we found ourselves returning regularly to a particular topic: how to motivate our kids to see what needed to be done around the house (or in their schoolwork or extracurricular activities such as music lessons) and then do it with a cheerful attitude and zero nagging from us. We needed something that would weather even the busiest of seasons, like the one in which we found ourselves. Every time we talked about creating some sort of chart, the conversation would peter out because we both "couldn't even." We needed something with longevity that didn't require us to make yet another trip to the store for supplies.

Inspiration struck when Shaun remembered the gargantuan change jar in which he'd been dropping his extra pennies for years. I'm sure he intended to have them changed for bills at the bank one day, but I honestly think the Lord had been preparing that penny jar for "just such a time as this" because the use we devised for them has been worth more than anything those pennies could buy.

Shaun proposed that we employ elements we already had in our home—oodles of pennies and a few glass jars—to implement an incredibly simple and practical way to encourage our kids to make good choices—whether spiritual, interpersonal, academic, or chore-related. We wrote each child's name on a jar with a chalk pen and then placed the jars, along with a master penny jar, on our kitchen windowsill.

During an at-home date night, we sat down and typed out a list of behaviors that could earn pennies, a list of offenses that could lose them, and a list of rewards for which the pennies could be redeemed. We prayed over this new system and asked the Lord to bless it with success and us with the will to consistently apply it.

And then we announced to Ezra, Simon, and Della (our only children old enough at the time to understand the concept) that they would be receiving pennies for things like kind speech, finishing a book, memorizing Bible verses, going the extra mile (in any scenario), learning a piece of music, or simply being especially eager to help. They would lose pennies for the opposite: snark, whininess, and dragging their feet when given a task. The kids responded to the idea with enthusiasm, especially when they saw that screen time, special treats, and "stay-up-late time" were all included on the "rewards" column.

It took about a week for us to get into the swing of remembering to transfer pennies from the master jar to the kids' containers when they did something penny-worthy, but soon, with the kids' enthusiastic reminders, we had developed a rhythm of discipline and rewards that used nothing more than spare change and cast-off mason jars.

## Given, Not Owed

From the outset, we explained to our kids that they could not demand pennies for their behavior and that doing something helpful with an obviously calculated motivation (more pennies) might not produce the results they were hoping for. Instead, we told them we would look for moments of genuine thankfulness, charity, and diligence. Just like with the Gentleness Challenge (or any other situation in which we choose to be especially mindful of our choices and attitudes), we noticed our kids beginning to look for ways to contribute or uplift.

*From the outset, we explained to our kids that they could not demand pennies for their behavior and that doing something helpful with an obviously calculated motivation (more pennies) might not produce the results they were hoping for.*

My desire is for my children to see the value of what Mother Teresa calls doing "small things with great love," regardless of whether or not anyone ever notices.

The more we encouraged, high-fived, and tossed pennies into jars for positive things we overheard from another room or happened upon without the kids even knowing we were there, the more our children's diligence and thoughtfulness grew.

I've always been humbled by our kids' capacity for goodwill. They are all quick to accept newcomers, reach out to the marginalized, and celebrate the ignored. It's one of my favorite things about them. And one of my most grateful mothering moments to this day was when a fellow mom at our homeschool co-op messaged me to let me know she had noticed our two oldest boys playing basketball with a student who was often avoided because of his burn scars.

I knew our kids had great capacity for kindness. (Guess what? Yours do too.) But sometimes, as illustrated above, they are more willing to lavish that consideration on those they barely know over their own family. But as we forged ahead with the Penny Reward System, I saw this trend begin to shift. Their eyes had been opened to the joy of treating their siblings not just with civility but also with the same consideration with which they wanted to be treated. The result was increased harmony in our home and an ever-increasing penny pile. The kids loved receiving pennies both because they could "spend" them on rewards and because the pennies became a reward in themselves—evidence that their efforts had been noted and appreciated.

An important element to the success of this system is the intermittent nature of how we choose to issue pennies. Yes, we always award pennies for a finished book of a certain length. But for less concrete instances, we reserve the right to allot pennies in some instances and not in others, "as the spirit leads."

For example, it's long been our girls' job at bedtime to help their younger brothers get settled. They read them a story from the children's Bible and tuck them in. The little boys love it, and the girls enjoy being the preferred "tuck-in sister," but some days, one is more eager than the others to volunteer. We don't have a set day for each of them, so the task usually falls to the first to speak up. Many times, this results in a penny for the quickest to claim it, but not always. Not knowing whether they will get a penny for their actions keeps the focus on the action for its own sake. Perhaps even more crucial than the penny itself is the specific word of approval that we include. Pennies make our kids smile. Praise makes them beam!

Entitlement is a cancer that hollows out the core of even the most seemingly altruistic gestures. One thing I love about the flexibility of the Penny Reward System is that it allows the focus to remain on noticing genuine effort or empathy rather than enforcing the attitude of being owed, an attitude that would surely grow in our children if every mechanical good deed were given its "due." In a culture obsessed with "virtue signaling," my desire is for my children to see the value of what Mother Teresa calls doing "small things with great love," regardless of whether anyone ever notices or pats them on the head for it. For as 1 Corinthians 13:3 (ESV) says, "If I give away all I have, and if I deliver up my body to be burned, but have not love, I gain nothing."

## Motivation Matters

It's a lot to ask of some dirty copper coins and a sorry collection of smudged glass jars. But years later, we're still going strong with the PRS, and we've added several happy earners to our ranks. Honestly, I'm not surprised that we've been able to keep going, since the PRS has a straightforward style that's perfect for our family. Also, it's pennies, and what little kid doesn't love the idea of earning money—even money that can only be redeemed for privileges or treats?

What has surprised me a bit is just how impactful the idea of losing pennies has been on our kids. Because we have attached significance to the earning of a penny, the same meaning inherently clings to the loss of one as well. Our kids really don't like having their pennies taken away, not only because it reduces their "currency" but also because it's a visual representation of something they have chosen to say or do in a less than stellar way. They are sad to lose pennies because they know that it means they have not done their best as unto the Lord.

The culture of mediocre motherhood teaches that "bribing your kids to leave you alone" is standard. How else can you get a moment's peace? At the same time, I see many mothers concerned with not being able to give their kids what "they deserve" (things like name-brand shoes, the most coveted toys, and the most expensive education) from a material standpoint. Neither focus speaks to the heart of what the Bible teaches about what we deserve ("the wages of sin is death," as Romans 6:23 points out so clearly). Both fail to highlight the importance of instilling and reinforcing godly character in our children, which is the only way to gain a peace that "surpasses all understanding" (Philippians 4:7 ESV). Not only that, but the emphasis on worldly goods only underscores that attitude of entitlement I mentioned earlier. We're all capable of falling into that trap, but children are especially prone to it, and it's our job as their mothers to lift their eyes from the world's riches and direct their gaze upon Jesus and others.

Rewards from the PRS are far from bribery, and they certainly don't afford more "me time." In fact, the most coveted prize for each of our older children is "stay-up time," so much so that we have designated Saturday night as "stay-up night," and the majority of our kids' pennies go toward their favorite night of the week when, if they have the pennies for it, they can stay awake two hours longer than usual doing the activity of their choice with Shaun and me.

Even as tired as I often am by the end of the week, I love that our kids view extra time spent with us as a treat. (Full disclosure: Their activities of choice are an interactive computer game with Shaun or a movie with me—we're not exactly learning wood carving or macramé here, people.)

## Following Jesus Is Its Own Reward

Over the years since I first introduced the PRS on my blog, it has emerged as one of the most asked about, replicated, and loved mothering hacks I have shared (ironic since it was dreamed up by a father). In fact, it's been in such demand that I wrote an e-book with exactly how we break our system down, since I was answering almost constant queries about it and the blog post I wrote left people wanting more specifics. As happy as it makes me to know that something so basic could be a blessing to other families as well as ours, what I truly hope you take away from this chapter is this:

1. If you feel overwhelmed by the thought of teaching your children to love to do the right thing, as unto the Lord, don't be! It doesn't have to be complicated. You don't really need a system at all, per se—just a desire and willingness

to keep bringing your children back to the well of Living Water that never runs dry. Should you still find yourself wanting something more practical, by all means, grab some pennies and a few jars. This is a setup that even the most free-spirited families can stick with.

2. If you already have a system complete with all the bells and whistles that make my skin crawl, I'm so proud of you! You're a rock star! As I've said, there are many, many ways to be a good mother, and having charts and stickers and organized prize closets is definitely one of them.

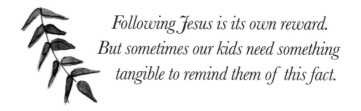

*Following Jesus is its own reward.*
*But sometimes our kids need something*
*tangible to remind them of this fact.*

Following Jesus is its own reward. But sometimes our kids need something tangible to remind them of this fact. It's up to us as their mamas to find ways to connect with their hearts and minds in order to bring the practical truths of Scripture to life. I love that Jesus uses the parable of the talents in Matthew 25 ("Well done, good and faithful servant") to give his followers a visual of the value of investing in God's kingdom. It makes me think he would have approved of the Penny Reward System too.

# THE PENNY REWARD SYSTEM FAQS

1. **Do kids start out with pennies in their jars?**

   They certainly can. It's encouraging to kids to begin with a bit of currency already in place. I suggest giving each child five pennies to start.

2. **How often do you award pennies?**

   We can go whole days without passing out any pennies, since our goal is to take genuine notice of "above and beyond" attitudes and actions. Some days, we might pass out as many as twenty. But we rarely give more than two pennies for any particular thing we notice. And it's usually just one.

3. **How much does each reward cost?**

   This can vary widely depending on how liberally you award pennies and what the activity is. But in our house, it costs a penny for ten minutes of screen time or stay-up time (the two most coveted rewards).

4. **How often can pennies be redeemed for rewards?**

   Once a day is a good guide. You can even set a reminder in your phone and let your kids know that they shouldn't be asking to redeem any rewards before that time. That said, as I mentioned above, other than "stay-up night," our kids' reward of choice is fifteen minutes of computer time, and they know not to ask until they are finished with their schoolwork. Some may not want their kids to redeem privileges more often than once a week. That is perfectly legitimate as long as you have kids with enough patience and forethought to think that far ahead.

5. **Do you have a master list of things for which you award pennies?**

   I do in the e-book I talked about. You can find it here: www.misfor mama.net/penny-reward-system.

WELL DONE GOOD AND FAITHFUL SERVANT

MATTHEW 25:23

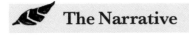 **The Narrative**

| MEDIOCRE MOTHERHOOD | CHRISTLIKE MOTHERHOOD |
|---|---|
| Chooses complaining over improvement | Looks for workable solutions |
| Gets overwhelmed and stays there | Gives the overwhelm to the Lord |
| Says "this won't work" | Believes with God all things are possible |

 **Action Steps**

- Memorize and meditate on Matthew 25:29 (ESV): "For to everyone who has will more be given, and he will have an abundance. But from the one who has not, even what he has will be taken away."

- Consider what "talents" the Lord has given you and whether you are stewarding them well for his glory.

- Choose a practical method to increase the peace in your home. Consider implementing the PRS or something similar as a way of encouraging and reminding your kids to choose wisely.

## Questions

Have I taken measures to create a peaceful atmosphere in our home, or am I flying by the seat of my pants?

Do I let comparison to others' methods paralyze my attempts to establish helpful systems in my home?

What are my strengths and weaknesses in this area? How can I improve?

## Prayer

*Lord, in the parable of the talents, you teach us to take the resources we've been given and multiply them for your kingdom. May we be willing to make the effort of finding out what works best to bring peace and order to our families so that we can glorify you.*

# Boot Camp Parenting

## CORRECTING BIG BAD HABITS
## WITH A BITE-SIZED APPROACH

The phrase "this too shall pass" used to baffle me. As a kid, it held zero meaning for my brain. As a teenager, it sounded mystical and deeply wise—if cryptic. And as an adult without children, it seemed true but distant.

But now, as a mama of ten, it is a lifeline, a veritable fount of empathy and hope in four syllables.

### Nothing Lasts Forever

Why? Because once you become a parent, there are phases that feel endlessly difficult until you finally emerge on the other side. I definitely found myself wishing away our firstborn's potty-training woes. And I couldn't wait to get through the debilitating nursing pain caused by Titus and Toby's tongue-tie issues. Since those are my first and my ninth and tenth children respectively, you might think that I never learned my lesson of "carpe dieming" every precious moment.

But the truth is that it's completely normal not to love a phase you're in when it's incredibly hard. I don't think that "rejoicing always" (Philippians 4:4) is the same as "enjoying always." I find no evidence that Jesus thought taking up his

I don't think that "rejoicing always" is the same as "enjoying always".

literal cross was fun—or that we're expected to think taking up our figurative crosses is a lark either. We can rejoice that God's strength is made perfect in our weakness when our eight-month-old is going through a brutal sleep regression. It doesn't mean that we have to do high kicks about the lack of sleep itself. In fact, I might check your temperature if you did.

At this point, when young moms ask me how I made it through the toddler tantrum phase, I point out two things: (1) I still have several kids who are in it, and (2) my perspective on it is very different than it was the first go-round because I now know that they will not melt down over butter on their butter knives (remember that?) forever.

*As much as the fact that not one phase lasts forever is balm for parents buckling under the weight of poopy diapers, sassy attitudes, and endless snack procuring, it's also a sobering reminder of just how little time we really have to teach our children and to delight in discovering who God made them to be.*

Of course, this knowledge is a double-edged sword. As much as the fact that not one phase lasts forever is balm for parents buckling under the weight of poopy diapers, sassy attitudes, and endless snack procuring, it's also a sobering reminder of just how little time we really have to teach our children and to delight in discovering who God made them to be. I often fight the urge to think, "All right! I'm done with this season. Next!" But then I remember with a bittersweet pang that my toddler's lisp won't last. My babies' delicious thigh rolls will dwindle as they become more active. And my twin girls won't need me to put their hair in "high shaky tails" much longer. At the time that I write this, I have two teenagers—fast-growing young men who are mere single-digit years away from flying the coop.

I never want my default to be "wishing away" any phase, even the hard ones, because I don't want to miss out on anything the Lord has to teach me or my children. But neither do I want to feel like a victim of my circumstances—because sometimes we find ourselves confronting behavior that more closely resembles a nasty bad habit than a standard developmental hiccup. And while, yes, the Lord uses our parenting shortcomings and our children's sinful choices to mold us, he has also given us the ability and the responsibility to face hard scenarios with courage and purpose.

## Simple, Not Easy

Too often, I receive messages that say something like "My daughter just won't eat what I make. But what can you do?" Or "My son will not do what I ask, no matter the consequences."

In these situations, a shrug and a simper over "the stage he's in" won't cut it. Even though it's human nature to test our limits, there is no guarantee that a stage of rebellion will not beget more rebellion if left unaddressed. For the mamas who write to me, the problem is rarely a lack of desire to see change but instead a feeling of not knowing where to start. I can relate. I've been there. Maybe we've let the snotty attitude go for so long that we feel like there's no hope respectful tones will ever return. Maybe we've allowed them to crawl into bed with us for 100 nights in a row, and we're resigned to the fact that three-year-old elbows in our ribs are *de rigueur* now.

Maybe we also know that while each season differs, we may well be facing a second verse very similar to the first with an older and bigger child if we don't just start somewhere. And yet we don't know where that somewhere is.

If any of this sounds familiar to you, it might be time for something I like to call "boot camp parenting." Before I ever gave it an official name, this simple practice of breaking tough parenting tasks down into manageable "bite-sized" goals had served me well for over a decade. Boot camp parenting is my go-to for everything from potty-training regression to mulish attitudes to keeping our car cleaned out.

If the term "boot camp" evokes images of toddlers doing burpees and tire runs, never fear. Boot camp parenting is (usually) low on physical exertion but high on mental perseverance. If, however, you're picturing a short time of focusing on a particular area of training, then you're on the right track.

Whenever we find ourselves facing a parenting quandary that feels overwhelming, Shaun and I have a conversation about what we need to do. First, we acknowledge that we have been lax in a particular area. Or maybe it's popped up seemingly out of nowhere, and we want to address it before things get really sticky. Either way, our approach is the same: We sit down and prayerfully outline several simple steps we will repetitively take to address the issue for one week.

That's it. One week of concentrated effort in one area. It sounds so simple—and it is—but depending on how entrenched the behavior is that we're dealing with, it's still not easy. Nor is this a magic, one-size-fits-all pill that works for every scenario. (Case in point: We worked with one of our kids on his finger-sucking habit for months before we found a solution.) But it is a useful parenting tool to have in your repertoire, one that often makes a task you've been dreading feel doable if not downright easy.

## One Week to More Peace

Maybe your two-year-old needs to learn how to say "please" and "thank you."

Maybe your four-year-old has gone from sleeping all night to waking up and trying to get in bed with you every night.

Maybe your eleven-year-old needs constant reminders to choose joy.

Maybe your fourteen-year-old has developed a bad habit of picking at her acne.

All these issues, while undesirable, are hardly deal breakers. And that's what "boot camp parenting" is best for—helping correct bad habits in a manageable amount of time and a lasting way.

Often, the biggest hang-up in addressing problematic behavior in our children is not the behavior itself—at least not on their part. It's our lack of follow-through.

I'll illustrate what I mean with a message I received from a mom who wanted to know how to apply boot camp parenting to her bedtime frustrations. She told me that getting her four small boys to go to bed was draining enough on its own. But then every night, without fail, they would take turns emerging from their upstairs room with requests for water, an observation about the weather, or a complaint about being pummeled or ambushed in bed.

It was like bedtime whack-a-mole.

"Just when I've finally managed to relax at the end of a long day, they keep asking for anything and everything to stay awake, and it's threatening my sanity," she said.

I've received dozens of similar messages and have experienced exactly the same scenario in my own home, so I asked her how she responded.

"I yell at them to go to bed from downstairs because I'm just too tired to get up and deal with it. But that usually makes it worse."

Again, I get it. I think we've all gone through something remarkably similar as mothers. But the irksome truth is that our kids very quickly figure out when we are "too tired to get up and deal with it," and they will use this knowledge to their advantage whenever possible.

I asked her if she was willing to try something different for one week, and she assured me she was. These are the steps I suggested:

1. Prepare your kids for bedtime by letting them know exactly what you expect of them and exactly what will happen if they don't obey.

2. Remind them that once they go to their rooms, they will not be allowed to come out for something they forgot, so they'd better do XYZ now. (Sometimes the problem is something as simple as easily distractible munchkins who have good intentions but become so engrossed in their toothbrush sword fights that they forget the last swallow of water for the day, that swallow that every child the world over deems necessary for survival; in this case, it's our job as parents to jog their memories.)

3. Stand outside their door and calmly send back any child who attempts to worm his way through.

4. Provide discipline if outright belligerence rears its ugly head.

I gave her this advice based on our applying the exact same steps to very similar scenarios in our own home. I had no idea if she would follow through, but less than a week later, I had another message that said, "It's working! The first two nights, I had to stand at the door for 30 minutes and send them back to bed multiple times. But after that, I could just kiss them good night, tell them I would be outside, and then stay in the general vicinity for a few minutes to make sure they didn't try to escape. I haven't had to do anything for the last two nights, and it's amazing how much more relaxed our nighttime routine is."

She went on to say that it wasn't even that hard but that she had been avoiding standing at the door for months because she'd been telling herself she was too exhausted to climb the stairs. Once she did it, though, she realized just how much of a toll the stress of anticipating the nightly bedtime battle was taking on her nerves and wished that she'd tackled the problem head-on months before.

*Boot camp parenting is as much about training ourselves to put in the hard work of mothering well in intensive scenarios as it is about shaping our children's habits.*

Just like with training our kids in long-term frameworks, boot camp parenting is as much about training ourselves to put in the hard work of mothering well in intensive scenarios as it is about shaping our children's habits. When we gird our spiritual loins with the fruit of the Spirit (most notably patience, kindness, and self-control) and wade into the fray of correcting harmful habits rather than sitting by in despair, we will find that we have improved not just our children's behavior but also our own character. Because if we're honest, all too often "I'm too tired" masks our own lack of discipline or dedication (ask me how I know). The good news is that the boot camp benefits are available for all involved and have a wonderful spillover effect on the overall levels of peace in our home.

## Using the Discernment God Gave Us

One thing I've noticed is that many mamas want a prescriptive approach to tackling frustrating behavior. "Okay," they'll say, "that worked for a passel of boys who kept getting out of bed, but what about a twenty-three-month-old who won't stop whining?" (You might think I'm joking about the specificity of the age; I'm not.) "What about a snarky twelve-and-a-half-year-old girl?" (Again with the exact age and gender in this case.)

I understand how incredibly convenient it would be to open our magic carpetbag, and out pops our own personal Mary Poppins to rattle off the perfect recipe for tantrum taming, complete with a crisp British accent and a catchy tune. But Scripture, especially Proverbs, makes it clear that parenting is much more about godly principles than exact prescriptions. Even more important, it stresses how crucial it is to seek God's truth above man's.

Proverbs 2:6 (ESV) says, "For the LORD gives wisdom; from his mouth come knowledge and understanding." Yes, it's helpful to reach out to women who are farther down the mothering road, but there is still no guarantee that they will have encountered our exact parenting crisis or even have sound advice on its particulars. I never want anything I suggest to replace a mother's need to seek God's direction in every area of her life—including the thirty-three-month-old who yodels in his sleep (okay, I made that up).

We must develop a habit of entreating the Lord to show us which areas would be worthy of addressing in a concentrated way and which ones are more of a "slow and steady" situation. He never fails to give wisdom when we ask, whether that's how we should proceed or whom we should contact for help.

A couple more disclaimers about the boot camp parenting approach:

1. None of us gets more than twenty-four hours in a day. So no matter how tempting it may be to attempt to grapple with multiple "boot camp" issues at once, we must resist the urge—for the sake of our sanity and our household equilibrium. If we are forever harping on one issue after another all day long,

FOR THE *Lord* GIVES WISDOM

PROVERBS 2:6

our children will begin to feel like a fixer-upper project rather than a source of joy. If you feel like you could "boot camp" seven different things at once, join the club. Take a deep breath. They'll still be there when you're done training your kids to close the back door. Or they will have worked themselves out on their own while you were focused elsewhere, in which case they weren't worth your extra attention in the first place.

2. There are issues that will take much longer than a week to address. My girl twins didn't grow out of certain sensory issues for eighteen months. And we spent a good two years teaching one of our boys to deal with his tendency to turn into a "rage monster."

That's perfectly normal. Not every parenting pothole we encounter will be as easily navigable as the last. Some may be mere jolts in the road to peace in our homes. Others may feel like pits so deep we can never climb out. But God in his mercy is faithful to steward us through each phase that comes our way as we look to him for wisdom and the strength to survive even the toughest weeks of parenting boot camp.

## BOOT CAMP PARENTING CHEAT SHEET

1. Explain what you expect of your kids for that week.

2. Talk about that week's goal often. Give lots of reminders and encouragement. Keep that issue at the forefront of your daily admonishments.

3. Provide practical support (standing at the bedroom door, being ready with the potty treat, supervising every detail of a toy cleanup, and so on).

4. Discipline/reward immediately; swift feedback is *key*.

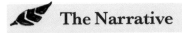 **The Narrative**

| MEDIOCRE MOTHERHOOD | CHRISTLIKE MOTHERHOOD |
|---|---|
| Sidesteps chronic behavioral issues | Addresses bad habits with intentionality |
| Thinks that "hard" is a good reason to quit | Knows that "hard" is not the same thing as "bad" |
| Focuses on self-pity | Focuses on what's best for the family as a whole |

 **Action Steps**

- Memorize and meditate on Proverbs 29:17 (ESV): "Discipline your son, and he will give you rest; he will give delight to your heart."
- Take the time to evaluate hard kid situations to determine whether they are merely phases or full-blown bad habits.
- Lay out specific "boot camp" parenting strategies for the areas that qualify as bad habits.

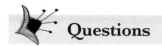 **Questions**

What is keeping me from addressing problem areas (fear, laziness, overwhelm, distraction...)?

What am I willing to sacrifice to help my kids overcome struggles with bad habits?

What does digging in and doing the hard work of parenting say to my kids?

 **Prayer**

> *Lord, nothing compares with the "hard" of the cross. Please make us mindful of those areas that require focused attention and give us perseverance to not "grow weary of doing good" (Galatians 6:9 ESV).*

# 13

# Cultivating a Peaceful Home

## CONSTANT FIGHTING DOESN'T
## HAVE TO BE THE NORM

My brother and I fought a lot. Not just verbally either. We would have what we Southerners like to call "knock-down, drag-outs." I can distinctly remember my mom's going to the grocery store when we were old enough to be left alone (although what I'm about to tell you would make anybody question if that were really true), and we would invariably get into it over—who knows what. It could have been anything. He liked to call me "Goober," which infuriated me. Sometimes that's all it took. He was naturally pesky, and I was naturally feisty. We were a match made in bickering heaven.

Except, as I mentioned, we didn't just bicker. He would pin me down and tickle me. Forcefully. I would writhe and scratch and slap. It would deteriorate from there. I might have jabbed a pencil into his leg after he threatened me with scissors one too many times. (In my defense, I did warn him. Okay, there is no defense.)

It was a mess. But in some ways, it's just how we related to each other at that age. And in other ways it wasn't really like us because we were pretty well-behaved, obedient types who got along quite a bit of the time too.

Eventually—praise Jesus—we aged out of our WWE days without actually maiming each other. By the time I was ten and he was fourteen, we were the best of buds. I have so many happy memories of tagging along to all of my big bro's events, blasting the radio and belting out '90s grunge tunes that we weren't really supposed to be listening to (sorry, Mom—guess we weren't *that* obedient), jamming together in our Christian grunge band (yeah, you read that right), playing endless games of "slaughter ball" and pickup basketball with our youth group, and even carpooling to community college together. I could hear his voice saying "Goober" from across a crowded room and smile instead of seeing red.

## Disagreement Versus Strife

Maybe parts of our story sound familiar, since sibling rivalries and tensions permeate much of any family's narrative. To some extent, they are an inevitable part of growing up as our kids wade deeper into the waters of adult conflict resolution and personality differences. However, there is a difference between normal levels of disagreement and constant strife.

Romans 12:18 (BSB) exhorts us, "If it is possible on your part, live at peace with everyone." I love that phrase, "on *your* part." In other words, simply saying, "But he started it," won't cut it. Especially since verse 17 says, "Do not repay anyone evil for evil." Even if he *did* start it, the Bible makes it clear that we're not supposed to finish it.

And yet "finishing it" is the number one thing that my kids want to do in their sinful flesh. Me too! (Don't forget that pencil-jabbing episode.) But circling back around to the beginning chapter of this book, just because something is relatable does not mean that it's not a completely mediocre, downright wrong response. So even though I understand that urge to "get mine in," it is still *my job* to teach my children the art of living at peace with *all* "men." (And yes, kids, that includes your brothers and sisters.)

LIVE at PEACE
with everyone
ROMANS 12:18

*The difference between mediocre motherhood and biblical motherhood is that one accepts— even laughs at—the inevitable with snarky memes, and the other creates strategies for learning how to overcome it peacefully in Christ's strength.*

Worldly culture teaches that kids will fight, that there's no avoiding discord. So we might as well grit our teeth and struggle through it. And there's some truth in that. If the fact that our children don't always get along is enough to unseat us, we're in for quite a bumpy ride. But the difference between mediocre motherhood and biblical motherhood is that one accepts—even laughs at—the inevitable with snarky memes, and the other creates strategies for learning how to overcome it peacefully in Christ's strength.

Those memes may be hilarious and "truth" filled, and I've been known to laugh at the more accurate portrayals of "typical" sibling behavior, but to dwell in this response is to ignore the transformational power of Scripture.

## Scripture Actually Works

After reading some of my Instagram highlights about how to quell sibling spats, a reader once asked me for "things that actually work," adding, "don't just give me Bible verses because that's not realistic." I understood what she meant. She wanted practical action steps. "When Hudson calls Sara a rude name, and she responds by slapping him, I _____."

But the fact is almost all our family's conflict action steps are steeped in Bible truth, which teaches us the reason for our sin and what to do about it.

James 4:1-3 (ESV) says,

What causes quarrels and what causes fights among you? Is it not this, that your passions are at war within you?...You covet and cannot obtain, so you fight and quarrel. You do not have, because you do not ask. You ask and do not receive, because you ask wrongly, to spend it on your passions.

Did you catch both the underlying cause and the action steps embedded in those three verses?

Why do we quarrel? Because we are selfish and want what others have. When we can't have the same, we attack and demand some for ourselves.

One of the things we work on from an early age with our kids is the concept of contentment with and thankfulness for what we already have. Before we go inside a store, we let our kids know ahead of time what we are there for and that even though we will be tempted to want just about everything that catches our eyes, we will not be giving in to impulse purchases. This works great for older kids who have heard it for years. But, man, is it an act of perseverance with little kids who have a severe case of the "gimmes." I mean, seriously. My five-year-old once cried because I wouldn't buy him a lint roller. When I asked him if he even knew what it was, he sobbed, "No, but I want it!"

It may seem easier to simply give in and buy the candy, doll, random action figure dude, or (ahem) lint roller, but the truth is that our consistent acquiescence trains our kids to want something different—and more of it—every time we step inside a store. We may have avoided one checkout catastrophe, but we have also fed the More Monster that lives inside us all and paved the way for future confrontation in the process. On the other hand, when we remind our children of all the good things that we already have at home and encourage them to thank God for allowing them to play with the random action figure dude waiting for them in the bathtub, we are instilling habits of self-control and gratitude that when nurtured carefully, blossom into generosity.

Of course, it's not simply our covetousness that gets us into trouble. Have you ever encountered a child who clearly wants something but refuses to actually ask for it? I remember a mom from the exercise group I host who instructed Ezra and Simon *not* to give her son a cookie—that he clearly wanted but was too shyly stubborn to actually ask for—until he gave in and used his words. What a strange paradox! "You do not have because you do not ask." We want something, and in some cases, that's not a bad thing. But we end up throwing a fit or getting in a fight simply because we refuse to give polite voice to our desire.

Hang on, Abbie. It doesn't actually say anything about being polite.

Doesn't it, though?

"You ask and do not receive because you ask wrongly."

How many times have we all witnessed a "say please" fight? You know what I'm talking about: One child wants a glass of milk, and the other is zealously guarding the fridge door because his brother just won't "say please." It's almost comical—but not—because the heated emotions are very real. So much friction could be avoided in our homes if we would all just express ourselves with the same kindness and cordiality with which we'd like to be addressed. And yet pushing past that lump of pride to humble ourselves before our peers—be they siblings, coworkers, friends, or spouses—and just ask kindly, rather than take, can require a monumental effort.

And finally, we ask and do not receive because we "ask wrongly, to spend it on [our] passions" (James 4:3 ESV). When it comes to my younger kids, this is often manifested in an epic Lego smackdown that starts with one child's demand for the Darth Vader head to place atop his mailman's body—not because it makes any sense whatsoever but because it gives him control over the most coveted Lego noggin in the entire bin. His selfish passions drive him to create strife even when no logic exists in the request.

Whoa. That was a lot to derive from one small snippet of Scripture, right? But that's what I love about the Bible! It's not "just theoretical" but is rich and nuanced in its practicality as well. Every time I read it, I notice something I missed the other fifty times I read the very same passage.

So when I tell you that our efforts to create peace in our home start with Scripture, I am not at all espousing some sort of ethereal philosophical theory.

Because of James 4, we start by practicing contentment and gratitude with what we have, which helps us avoid picking fights with our brother just because he has something we want. And then, if we still want or need it, we ask with

So much friction
could be avoided in our homes if
we would all just express ourselves
with the same kindness and cordiality
with which we'd like to be
addressed.

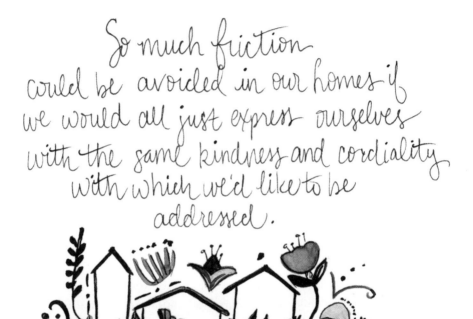

words that honor and uplift instead of humiliate and tear down. And finally, when we receive what we have asked for, we use it rightly in a way that glorifies God.

Or at least that's the goal. And we often fall short.

But let me tell you this: A righteous, Scripture-informed effort, even if imperfectly executed, will always produce more peace than an apathetic, self-focused one.

## Do Nothing from Selfish Ambition or Conceit

Of course, not all dissension arises from a desire for things. Sometimes it's the result of plain old personality differences. A couple of my kids get along with each of their siblings, no matter the combination or situation. A couple of others tend to produce, shall we say, more fireworks. Regardless of the personalities involved, though, we stress that we are to treat one another with respect and honor. I have a couple of children who have an unfortunate tendency to belittle younger siblings, and I've had to remind them on more than one occasion that they were once that younger sibling's age and had many of the same traits that they find babyish or tiresome. Would they have liked to have been treated with condescension and disdain at that age? Or would they have wanted understanding and forbearance?

We all know the answer, but it doesn't mean we won't have to keep preaching this truth to our children (and ourselves) until we're blue in the face: "Do nothing from selfish ambition or conceit, but in humility count others more significant than yourselves" (Philippians 2:3 ESV).

That can be a hard word for a twelve-year-old boy when it comes to his seven-year-old sister. Or a mama when it comes to her husband, who gets more sleep than she does because he doesn't have the right equipment to feed the baby. Or how about a young wife when it comes to her mother-in-law? Because not every bit of confrontation in a home comes in the form of sibling fights, of course.

And yet all of us must (ahem) *confront* more truth from Philippians 2 if we are to grow in Christlikeness and maintain an atmosphere of peace in our homes because verse 14 says that we should "do everything without grumbling or arguing."

Everything.

Sharing our toys. Doing our brother's chore when Mom asks. Making our 14-millionth snack of the day. Scrubbing the toilet. Doing the math problems. Giving up the dang Darth Vader head.

## Making Fighting a Non-option

In a culture in which we are expected to shrug at habitual sibling strife (not merely occasional disagreement) as one of life's constants alongside death and taxes, the Bible calls us to a radical approach to diffusing conflicts. Our kids do not have to fight constantly, and the Bible gives us clear instructions about how to achieve peace in our homes.

*If your goal is a peaceful home from the beginning, then it's imperative to nip bickering in the bud before it has the chance to become a well-worn family dynamic.*

Just as with every other aspect of training, teaching them to forgo constant picking and fussing requires first setting that example yourself and then consistently enforcing it day after sacred day. My Instagram friend Jodi Mockabee has a phrase that I love: "Start as you mean to go on." In other words, if your goal is a peaceful home from the beginning, then it's imperative to nip bickering in the bud before it has the chance to become a well-worn family dynamic.

*When fighting is not an option in our homes,*
*our children discover other ways to*
*communicate their differences.*

When fighting is not an option in our homes, our children discover other ways to communicate their differences. I once had a reader ask me how I expected my children to develop conflict resolution skills if I never allowed them to disagree. That would be a great question if I really did mean that making fighting a non-option is the same thing as outlawing disagreement. But the truth is that while I don't expect my children to always agree on what movie to watch or which dessert to bake or whose turn it is to do the dishes, I *do* expect them to be able to hash it out in a civil manner with the understanding that since *they* don't like being verbally or physically attacked, they will not inflict that same treatment on their siblings.

It is yet another practical application of pure Scripture, for the Golden Rule is no mere pithy proverb but instead an exhortation from Christ himself to "do to others what you would have them do to you" (Matthew 7:12). Do they always remember this rule? Nope. But when they do forget, there are consequences that are both appropriate and timely. For small children, this often means time spent in their rooms alone, since those who treat others unkindly forgo the privilege of being around others—at least for a time.

For my older kids, the Penny Reward System helps them stay on track. As I've already said, their preferred method of penny redemption involves paying for "stay-up time" on Saturday nights. And since the quickest way to earn a penny is unprompted kindness in speech or deed, the speediest way to *lose* one is picking fights. After all, who wants to stay up extra late with a contentious sibling?

Believe it or not, although my kids don't interact with each other cordially all the time, they do a decent job of checking themselves—and each other—whenever the urge to squabble arises. I've stifled a chuckle in my upstairs laundry room upon hearing the kids downstairs during our morning or evening pickup times telling each other in no-nonsense tones to "Stop bickering, or you'll lose stay-up night."

In addition to swift and consistent consequences, we also emphasize that we treat one another as we would like to be treated not just to benefit ourselves or to earn privileges but because it is the primary way that we can show family members and others our love for Christ.

"By this all people will know that you are my disciples, if you have love for one another" (John 13:35 ESV) should *start* with our own family members. So when I am admonishing my kids to "be a blessing" to each other while the toddler is getting on everyone's last nerve or the teenager is extra surly, I often ask them *why* we love others, to which they are known to respond with a begrudging "because he first loved us" (1 John 4:19). Begrudging not because they don't believe it's true, but *because* it is so true that there is zero wiggle room for excuse making or blame casting. Not only that, but the opportunities for cheering each other on are endless. So why not take advantage of those instead?

I'm under no delusion that we will ever eradicate every form of strife in our home. We won't be cured of the urge to "be right no matter what" until we reach glory. But following the precepts of Scripture makes it possible to achieve an environment of consistent camaraderie and encouragement, and I am always heartened when I hear words of genuine, unprodded praise flowing from my children's mouths.

Of course, one of the most important tools that helps build an atmosphere of peace in our home involves something we *don't* do. And it is informed by Scripture as well. I'll talk about it more in the next chapter, but let's just say that it's a lot easier to "be nice" to your siblings when you fill your mind and heart with examples of goodwill rather than snark.

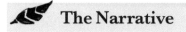 **The Narrative**

| MEDIOCRE MOTHERHOOD | CHRISTLIKE MOTHERHOOD |
|---|---|
| Shrugs at the "reality" that kids will habitually fight | Believes that while all kids can fight, it doesn't have to be constant |
| Copes with strife at home by defaulting to snark | Recognizes that Scripture always trumps snark |
| Uses nagging and bribery to achieve temporary peace | Focuses on addressing the "heart issue" in conflict |

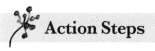 **Action Steps**

- Memorize and meditate on Proverbs 17:1 (ESV): "Better is a dry morsel with quiet than a house full of feasting with strife."

- Call a family meeting to lay out how you will deal with sibling strife going forward. Be specific about what qualifies as "bickering" or "unkindness" in your home.

- Enact a system like the PRS that will help your kids be mindful about their speech and actions as you either reward or discipline them.

 **Questions**

Have I fallen into the habit of believing that constant bickering is unavoidable? If so, why?

What factors have contributed when unkindness is on the uptick in my home?

How can I exemplify the truth that "we love because he first loved us"?

 **Prayer**

*Lord, we are way too good at doing "whatever seem[s] right in [our] own eyes" (Judges 21:25 NLT) without regard for how it affects other people. Help us to set the example of treating others in the way we want to be treated and to truly be at peace with everyone in our families and beyond.*

# 14

# We Are the Gatekeepers

## BECAUSE THE MEDIA WE CONSUME MATTERS

We probably all remember at least part of the children's song "O Be Careful, Little Eyes." It starts out with these words:

O be careful, little eyes, what you see
O be careful, little eyes, what you see
For the Father up above
Is looking down in love
So be careful, little eyes, what you see.

The rest of the verses end the same way but begin with slightly different encouragements:

Be careful, little ears, what you hear...
Be careful, little tongue, what you say...
Be careful, little hands, what you do...
Be careful, little feet, where you go...
Be careful, little heart, whom you trust...
Be careful, little mind, what you think...

The tune is childish, and the repetition can cause our minds to drift away from the truth of the words. But this song is profound, y'all. Not only does it manage to encapsulate the essence of dozens of Bible passages in a few short and simple verses, but it ends each refrain not with "for the Father up above is looking down waiting for you to mess up so he can squash you like a bug" but with "he is looking down with *love*." Sure, it fits into the rhythm of the stanza better, but it's also true. God cares about what we see, hear, say, trust, think, and do because he loves us too much to desire anything less than excellent things for us.

We can relate. We want the best for our children in every area. So why do we sometimes allow harmful and even downright destructive influences into their minds and hearts?

## Setting the Standard

I mentioned in the last chapter that I would talk about some of the things we choose *not* to do that help promote an atmosphere of peace and camaraderie in our home. One of the most essential is this: In the same way that we do not invite foul-mouthed, toxic, violent, or promiscuous people into our home to spend time with our children, we choose not to allow these people into our home through our television screens, books, or the music that we listen to.

Taking it a step further, we are careful with media that promotes mockery, discord, or cutting sarcasm. To some, our standards will seem excessive, archaic even. For others, the very fact that we have a television means that our benchmark is not high enough. What I am addressing here is not a universal standard for every home. But I *am* saying that every Christian home should have a standard for what they figuratively open their doors to.

A friend once told me that it wasn't until I had mentioned our attempts to avoid snarky shows as a way of promoting family harmony that it occurred to her that many of the shows her tween girls watched portrayed scene after scene of siblings who clearly considered each other a waste of space and oxygen. When she thought about her daughters' struggles to speak kind words to one another, something clicked, and she took those shows off of their regular watch rotation. She told me that without the influence of those shows, she saw rapid improvement in the civility of her girls' interactions.

*Mediocrity is stagnant. But excellence requires us to keep growing and evolving in Christlikeness, even if it doesn't look just like what our neighbors do.*

That is wise, proactive mama-ing right there. Mediocrity is stagnant. But excellence requires us to keep growing and evolving in Christlikeness, even if it doesn't look just like what our neighbors do.

Philippians 4:8 gives an idea of what our media goals should be: "Finally, brothers and sisters, whatever is true, whatever is noble, whatever is right, whatever is pure, whatever is lovely, whatever is admirable—if anything is excellent or praiseworthy—think about such things."

(Oy with the high standards, Paul.)

Herein lies one of the greatest divides between the culture of mediocre motherhood and biblically excellent parenting. The best I can tell, the gold standard for children's media in modern secularism includes cultural diversity, body positivity, self-love, and environmental advocacy. None of these issues is inherently evil (no, not even self-love, when the alternative is self-loathing), but each of them keeps the focus on created things (ourselves, the earth) rather than the Creator. As such, the way they are expressed often promotes self-obsession, identity politics, and—above all—an overlooking of sin. This approach tracks with a worldly view of morality, which mistakenly promotes "tolerance" as the highest form of love.

I once heard a pastor say something that stuck like a burr in my mind: "The most unloving thing we can do is watch someone walk down a path of destruction and do nothing to stand in their way." It's a radical concept in a culture that equates love with refraining from any judgment (or discernment) about the actions of others. And yet I might take his statement one step further to say that the most unloving thing we can do for our children is to *introduce* them to destructive influences and then allow them to follow that path to its logical conclusion.

## We Will Be Accountable

We are the gatekeepers of our homes. That means that we are ultimately accountable for the voices we allow to speak into our children's lives. Yes, we may be viewed as the "mean mom" if our kids aren't allowed to watch the seemingly harmless show that every other tween is obsessed with. But if we know the show to be full of innuendo, unbiblical agendas, and mockery, we cannot bow to the pressure of societal conformity. To do so would be to reinforce the concept that our peers' opinions matter more than our heavenly Father's. It would also rob us of a chance to show our kids what truly exceptional media looks like.

As their mamas, we have an incredible opportunity to introduce our children to life-giving, uplifting, thought-provoking books, shows, and music. Mediocre motherhood either bends under the pressure to fit in or never puts in the time to find better alternatives. I've actually heard the statement, "I can't stand this show, but it keeps them occupied, so I don't care." Christian mothers are fully aware of the relief a thirty-minute children's program can provide in our busy lives, but we must stand firm in our conviction that anything we allow our children to watch should be something that edifies their minds and hearts.

## Discernment Is the Thing

Again, I am not about to dictate specifics of the media that meets biblical criteria, although at the end of the chapter I will share some examples that our family has gotten value from for those who need ideas. I am aware that not everyone will agree with my suggestions. I remember talking about our family's enjoyment of the British animated show *Peppa Pig* once. Several mothers were disappointed that I would allow my little children to watch it, since Peppa sometimes exhibits disrespectful, bossy, self-centered behavior toward her friends and family. I couldn't argue. Peppa is hardly a paragon of thoughtfulness or humility. However, for our family, the constructive elements of the show— the cheerful family dynamic, the childlike nature of the storylines, the gentle humor and positivity—outweighed the times when we needed to stop and discuss why it was rude for Peppa to contradict Daddy Pig or to sass her friends. Unfortunately, this is no longer true. *Peppa Pig* now includes content that contradicts biblical values, and we have discontinued watching the show. This is a perfect example of why it's so important to diligently monitor the entertainment our family consumes. In an increasingly anti-God culture in which even children's shows promote agendas that undermine the Creator's clear design for family, it is our responsibility to preach the truth to our kids through the media we allow in our homes.

Another example would be for The Chronicles of Narnia or Tolkien's Lord of the Rings series. I have been challenged multiple times about the worthiness of any book that includes magical elements, given Scripture's warnings against fraternizing with the occult (see Leviticus 19:31, Isaiah 8:19, Micah 5:12, and others). But when I look at the purpose behind the references to fantastical elements in these books, it seems clear that they are meant to direct readers *to* Christ, not to exalt magic for its own sake. And so these two series are dear to our family's hearts.

Prayerful discernment and the opportunities for teachable moments are two of the things that help us decide as a family which media we will and won't consume. I don't require that the characters of our books *never* say an unkind word. I don't even require that they never use profanity. One of our favorite books to listen to in the car is *Little Britches*, which, in spite of being a wonderful example of good character-building stories in many ways, includes spurts of "mild" profanity when certain characters are speaking. Shaun and I view this as an opportunity to stop and discuss the motivation behind such language and why we choose to forgo it. Complex characters and stories about redemption (think Eustace in *The Voyage of the Dawn Treader*, Kalmar in The Wingfeather Saga, or Orual from *Till We Have Faces*) make some of the best family read-alouds. But there is a marked difference between a wrongly motivated character who learns the error of his or her ways (or even a rightly motivated character with a colorful vocabulary) and a tone of pervasive ridicule and insult, especially when it's passed off as expected or even acceptable.

# The Connection Between
# Consumption and Character

An acquaintance once described to me the struggles she was having with her son's contentious, scornful attitude. In almost the same breath, she mentioned that he was reading *Diary of a Wimpy Kid* and that she wasn't thrilled with some of the terminology and conduct in the books. Still, her conclusion was that "at least he's reading," without ever seeming to draw a connection between the kind of book he was internalizing and the kind of behavior he was exhibiting.

 *Sometimes we adopt the mindset that reading is wholesome for its own sake when it very much matters what we are reading.*

Sometimes we adopt the mindset that reading is wholesome for its own sake when it very much matters *what* we are reading. As a teenager, I consumed a great deal of Christian romance fiction, which, arguably, is heavy on schmaltz and light on theological substance. I read my fair share of Jane Austen and Dostoevsky and Dumas as well (I was an English major). But I wish now that I could time-travel back to my younger self, pluck the formulaic "faith fiction" book from her hands, and replace it with Zora Neale Hurston's *Their Eyes Were Watching God* or Alan Paton's *Cry, the Beloved Country*. Neither is strictly Christian, and yet both contain the kind of writing and character development that force readers to grapple meaningfully with right and wrong, good and evil.

This is not the case with many so-called young-adult novels, which often contain more gratuitous sex, violence, self-harming, and obscenities than several "adult" books combined. Because of their postmodern approach to morality, they seldom present a genuine example of good or evil but are instead merely peopled with anxiety-ridden individuals trying to discover "their truth."

I love what Sarah MacKenzie, author of *The Read-Aloud Family*, said on her podcast about this kind of fiction:

> All good books leave the reader seeing their world afresh...authors are duty bound to tell young readers the truth. The truth is HOPE. I have serious concerns about books leaving readers feeling depressed or bleak, and I'm doubly concerned when that reader is a teenager. There may be no worse time in life to leave a reader feeling hopeless, angsty, or depressed. A book that leaves a reader feeling like "is this all there is?" is not a good book.[4]

Clearly, the *kind* of knowledge we ingest matters more than that we simply have a constant stream of it—another distinction between a biblical worldview and the secular one, which merely says that "knowledge is power." Perhaps. But sometimes its power is the hold it has over us. We see this as early as the Garden of Eden when Eve fell for the seduction of knowing things that would make her "like God." And then again, in the New Testament, Jesus reminds us, "Where your treasure is, there your heart will be also" (Matthew 6:21). The media that capture our money, our time, and our attention will influence us more than we could possibly realize in the moment.

*The media that capture our money, our time, and our attention will influence us more than we could possibly realize in the moment.*

Not only that, but when we begin to love that which we shouldn't, it's easy to pass it off initially as a small vice with little power over us.

## When We Love the Wrong Thing

It brings to mind the allegorical story of Princess Amanda in the richly woven Kingdom Tales Trilogy (another worthy member of the genre of literature that references magic but exalts Christ). Known for her infectious joy, singing, and perfect aim with a throwing axe, the princess is loved by all her people. And then, one day, she discovers a dragon egg. She knows she is forbidden from keeping it, but keep it she does, tucking it away in a secret place. And when the dragon hatches, she continues to harbor it, feeding and protecting it, even as the hatchling grows stronger and more aggressive, and she grows more attached, more withdrawn from her friends, and more resentful of the rightful rules that outlaw her contraband. One day, when she discovers smoldering grass in a field, she realizes that her clandestine pet is no longer content to stay in hiding and has expanded in both girth and cunning. When the beast emerges into the clearing, Amanda realizes to her dismay that "it had grown even more, and she had not noticed how much." (Who else is seeing parallels to her own pet vices?)

Finally, Princess Amanda is forced to kill the animal or be killed by it. She slays the creature but not without great physical and emotional trauma.

The allegory concludes with these words: "So the princess discovered that when one loves a forbidden thing, one loses what one loves most. The truth is a hard won battle for each who finds it and is always gained by loss."

Princess Amanda's fixation on the wrong thing strips her of her community and her joy. It almost takes her very life. And I do not think it is too dramatic to say that there are things that come out of books and screens that can do the same.

## Guarding Their Innocence

The average age of exposure to pornography in America is now between nine and eleven years old. It may be younger by the time you read these words. The hypersexualization of children has become mainstream in programs on Netflix and other popular streaming services. At an age when our daughters and sons should be climbing trees, playing with stuffed animals, and soaping down their trampolines for an extra thrill—because they are *children*—they are instead being inundated with terms like "twerking" and "motorboating" and images of performers stripping and pole dancing during the Super Bowl halftime show.

And that's if we're blessed enough to shield them from worse. (For the record, we have not watched the Super Bowl halftime show in years—certain choices are just too easy *not* to make.)

Guarding our children's innocence has never been trickier. It can often feel like we need a special parenting sixth sense that detects filth on its way to our children's eyes from miles away since so much of their exposure to purity-stealing junk will come from the devices of their peers. We can't protect them from everything. But their vulnerability should never result from our laxness or—God forbid—intentional neglect.

I would love to say that as mothers, we can all agree it's never okay to deliberately expose our children to content that will pollute their impressionable minds, promote secretive behaviors, and warp their view of future intimacy and their own self-worth. And yet hundreds of exploitative channels on YouTube would call me a naive fool. Greed is the ultimate mediocre—nay, reprehensible—mothering motivator, and there is mega money to be made in "pimping out" one's fresh-faced preteen daughters. Momagers who post videos of their eleven-year-olds writhing to sexually explicit songs in micro-mini skirts and plunging crop tops that barely cover their budding figures deserve jail time as far as I'm concerned. But instead, we are told that this is "normal" and that these "all-American" girls—who should still be playing with their American Girl dolls—have the maturity to understand the differences in how they should act depending on whether the camera's eye is blinking red. (Hint: Blinking or not, the scant clothes and suggestive dance moves should never happen.)

Here's the truth straight from Jesus's mouth: "For out of the heart come evil thoughts—murder, adultery, sexual immorality, theft, false testimony, slander. These are what defile a person" (Matthew 15:19-20). We cannot just switch off the sin that lives within us. Just like Princess Amanda's dragon, it will feed off of our refusal to name it, bring it into the light, and put it to death. It will grow until we realize we can no longer control it (as if we ever really could). Sadly, this truth applies to children as well. But Jesus also made it very clear what he thought of anyone who corrupts an innocent when he declared that "it would

It's our job as mamas to make our children's realities more enticing than any online world into which they might be tempted to flee.

be better for them to be thrown into the sea with a millstone tied around their neck than to cause one of these little ones to stumble" (Luke 17:2).

## The No-Phone Zone

In light of this dire warning, another thing that we do *not* do is allow our children to have their own electronic millstones—*er,* phones—before driving age, and even then, they do not have easy access to search engines, image sharing, or social media. The pitfalls of early exposure to the addictive and reality-twisting world of Instagram, Facebook, Snapchat, and others have been well documented with links to a rise in young users' levels of bullying, depression, suicide, likelihood to be preyed upon by pedophiles, and pornography exposure.

Not only that, but personal screens have been proven to have an isolating effect on young (okay, and not so young) users. The allure of their bright colors, endless apps, games, and pinging message alerts often proves overwhelmingly seductive to a ten-year-old for whom the alternative is something as low-tech as four square in the sunshine. Don't misunderstand me: Four square beats the pants off of *Fortnite* every day of the week. But unless we are willing to swim against the stream of a culture that paints tech obsession as an inevitable aspect of twenty-first-century childhood, our children might never have the opportunity to experience the magic of a well-placed, single-handed four square ball slam as shafts of summer sunlight beat down on sun-bleached mops of sweaty hair.

According to a *Forbes* article on tech addiction, "America's obsession with smartphones has even been compared to the obesity epidemic. That's because, just like drug or gambling addictions, smartphones provide an escape from reality."[5]

## Let's Make Reality Cool Again

It's our job as mamas to make our children's realities more enticing than any online world into which they might be tempted to flee. Good books, cookie baking, game playing, hymn singing, one-on-one dates, dance parties, s'mores around the firepit, music lessons, leaf-pile jumping—the list goes on. Besides

IF ANYONE
LOVES THE
WORLD,
LOVE FOR THE
FATHER
IS NOT IN THEM.

1 JOHN 2:15

limiting their physical access to virtual reality, we must be willing to put in the effort to help our kids realize just how much better real life is.

But most importantly, we must be devoted to instilling in them a love for a reality that we cannot yet see with our eyes—that of heaven and eternity with our Creator. As 1 John 2:15 says, "Do not love the world or anything in the world. If anyone loves the world, love for the Father is not in them." Simply introducing our children to the delights of this world will not suffice. But when we teach them to "taste and see that the Lord is good" (Psalm 34:8), we lay a foundation of conviction that can withstand even the most alluring online attractions.

It may be a revolutionary approach in a day and age when screens are the ultimate easy babysitters, and so many parents seem to believe that their children will not be able to keep pace with their peers, socially or academically, without them. I know too many mothers who truly believe that their seven-year-old will hate them forever if they deny them the "right" to technology, a right rife with responsibilities and repercussions that their young minds can't even begin to grasp. But I want to encourage every mama everywhere that neither your elementary-age child nor your tween—nor even, *gasp*, your teen—*needs* a smartphone with unfettered access to the internet.

If protecting my children and promoting unity in my home is revolutionary, then hand me a tricorn hat and call me Paul Revere. This is a book about rebelling against the culture of "mediocre motherhood" for a reason. Sometimes, keeping our children off the path of destruction means being willing to combat "what everybody else is doing" with Truth with a capital T (that's Jesus).

Yes, it's easier in the short term to hand our children a screen with the most popular show of the moment when we need a break, but easier is not necessarily better, and hard is not the same thing as bad. In fact, it is often our hardest mothering seasons that bear the most fruit in the long run. And it is the hard-won fruit—like the kind we harvest when we choose *not* to keep the technology status quo—that tastes the sweetest.

 **The Narrative**

| MEDIOCRE MOTHERHOOD | CHRISTLIKE MOTHERHOOD |
|---|---|
| Lets kids choose the media without vetting it | Does the research before allowing media into the home |
| Fails to recognize the lasting damage that ungodly media can inflict | Understands how impressionable young hearts and minds are |
| Uses screens as de facto babysitters | Stays engaged |

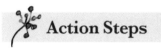 **Action Steps**

- Memorize and meditate on Romans 12:2 (ESV): "Do not be conformed to this world, but be transformed by the renewal of your mind, that by testing you may discern what is the will of God, what is good and acceptable and perfect."

- Commit to researching any media before you allow it in your home and to discussing teachable moments.

- Make a plan for how you will prepare your kids to respond rightly to the inevitable ungodly media sources they will encounter elsewhere.

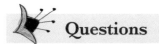

## Questions

What are some biblical standards for media every Christian home should abide by?

Do I apply these same standards to myself as well as my children? Why or why not?

How can I be a more effective gatekeeper of my own home?

## Prayer

*Lord, you say in 1 Corinthians 15:33 (ESV) that "bad company ruins good morals." Help us to be mindful of the "company" we keep in the media we allow into our homes. May we stay faithful to your standards of truth and purity, no matter how unpopular.*

# The Birds and the Bees

## TEACHING OUR KIDS ABOUT GOD'S GOOD DESIGN FOR SEX

Few things get parents blushing—regardless of their worldview—more than having to talk to their kids about sex. No matter how much we enjoy the act ourselves, describing the mechanics of it to, well, anyone can be more than a little uncomfortable. The discomfort increases exponentially when we're faced with the prospect of explaining sex to our own offspring, who will inevitably cringe at the epiphany that "Mom and Dad did *that* to have me." (Or, more to the point, Mom and Dad *still* do that.)

### Having "The Talk"

Based on an inbox full of messages begging for resources on how to approach the topic, it seems Christian mamas are especially flummoxed by the concept of having "the talk." (The mere fact that we have euphemisms like "the talk" is an indication of just how intimidating we find discussing sex with our kids.) And though I understand the panic (I confess to having been a little antsy the first time I had this conversation with one of our kids), the truth is that we can rest easy in the knowledge that the *only* thing God did not call good in his creation was the fact that Adam was alone. In fact, he said it was *"not* good." Woman was no afterthought, though. No, God gave Adam the opportunity to discover for himself that there was no soulmate for him among the animals, which only increased his wonder when he was given a "bone of my bones and flesh of my flesh" (Genesis 2:23) companion that was literally made for him and from him. God had a plan for intimacy between men and women long before they were faced with the prospect of outlining "the birds and the bees" for their kids.

*God had a plan for intimacy between men and women long before they were faced with the prospect of outlining "the birds and the bees" for their kids.*

## Redeeming "Sex Ed"

And because God's plan for sexuality in Scripture is so clear (and so good), we have to look no further than the Bible for a guide on how to pass along that information to our kids in a way that conveys the facts without requiring them to do anything weird to a banana.

Speaking of which, the "sex ed" available in schools too often focuses solely on the mechanics of the act or on the prevention of pregnancy and STIs, instead of on the beautiful design of "leaving and cleaving" that Genesis 2:24 outlines. Or at least that is what "sex ed" used to do. More and more, schools are using the class as an indoctrination tool that inundates even the youngest children with age-inappropriate details, alternative sexual orientations, and "tolerance training."

I wouldn't expect anything different from a culture that has strayed so far from its Judeo-Christian roots that the mere declaration that set genders are a biological fact, rather than a fluid "identification process," is considered discrimination. Just ask J.K. Rowling. Despite making references to "faith" and "religion," Rowling has waffled on a variety of topics, from whether life exists after death to what exactly defines good and evil. She was heartily embraced by secular culture and a band of rabid acolytes who idolize her Harry Potter series—until she made the seemingly innocuous "mistake" of saying that she believed in male and female genders.

> *As bizarre as it seems to become a "cancel culture" target simply for saying that boys are boys and girls are girls, this is the illogical conclusion of a society bent on rejecting even the most basic biblical standards.*

Suddenly, she was *persona non grata,* and her name was being scrubbed from as many literary surfaces as possible. As bizarre as it seems to become a "cancel culture" target simply for saying that boys are boys and girls are girls, this is the illogical conclusion of a society bent on rejecting even the most basic biblical standards. (Genesis 5:2 says, "He created them male and female and blessed them. And he named them 'Mankind' when they were created.")

Being aware that non-Christians will approach sexual topics from an unbiblical perspective and will even attempt to "cancel" those who disagree is not the same thing as accepting their conclusions. One of the defining characteristics of mediocre motherhood is passivity—a go-with-the-flow mentality that assumes we can do nothing to combat cultural mores, no matter how arbitrary or explicitly harmful they are. This mindset abdicates the God-given responsibility each mother has to root every aspect of her children's education—yes, sex education too—in his principles. This means that we do not leave the explanation of God's design for physical intimacy up to schools or television shows or peers. Doing so might spare us some embarrassment in the short term, but confronting uncomfortable scenarios is intrinsic to our job descriptions as mothers, and we must be willing to prioritize our children's long-term benefit over our own comfort.

Instead of allowing society to define the sexual terms that our children learn, we look to what Scripture has to say on the topic and engage with our children accordingly. And what it has to say is this: "Flee from sexual immorality. Every other sin a person commits is outside the body, but the sexually immoral person sins against his own body" (1 Corinthians 6:18 ESV). Secularism says that our bodies are ours to do with as *we* please. But Christianity understands that as a created being, man has one chief end—"to glorify God and enjoy him forever," as the Westminster Catechism puts it. Or as 1 Corinthians 6:19-20 says, "Do you not know that your bodies are temples of the Holy Spirit, who is in you, whom you have received from God? You are not your own; you were bought at a price. Therefore honor God with your bodies."

## A Practical Approach

Conveying what this means practically to our kids can look different for every family. But for ours, this looks like a special birthday trip when our kids turn ten. Shaun takes the boys, and I take the girls. We both discuss sensitive topics with them, but for this trip, sharing the same gender as the birthday honoree just makes sense.

When I did this with our oldest daughter, Della, we booked a visit to Dallas, which is a few hours away from our home. We reserved a fancy hotel room. We ate yummy food, talked, shopped, got our nails done, and watched British TV shows in our pajamas. The goal of the birthday trip was twofold: (1) to lavish undivided attention on Della and (2) to explain to her the particulars of something that she had been learning bits and pieces of for years.

Our family has read the Bible using *The One Year Bible* multiple times through the years, and we never skip or water down the passages that reference the sexual aspects of certain story lines. I know this is a controversial choice, but I grew up with parents who also read the Bible to me as it was written. As a result, by the time I was ten years old, I was aware of many aspects of human sexuality simply because they had been mentioned in a daily Bible passage, and

Honor God with your Bodies

1 Corinthians 6:20

I had asked questions. I didn't always get the full answer, and neither do our younger children.

Let's say we've just read the account of Dinah being assaulted by Shechem in Genesis 34. If our five-year-old asks what "rape" is, we explain that rape is when a man hurts a woman badly, and it is very wrong. As our kids mature and learn more about the specifics of sex, we are able to add nuance to this explanation. The same goes for phrases like "Adam *knew* his wife." It's not necessary to spell out the details to a young child, but we can say this does not just mean that Adam knew who Eve was but that it refers to something God gave specifically to married people. Again, as their knowledge expands, we are able to use our discernment about when to peel back more layers of protective ignorance until, when they are ready, they have a full biblical understanding of sex.

## Our Kids Can Handle It

In Della's case, she was aware that her older brothers had received special knowledge on their tenth-birthday trips, so she was expecting a discussion of some sort. And she was utterly matter-of-fact as we had it. Too often, we underestimate our children's ability to absorb and assimilate information at face value. Yes, the response will vary depending on the child's personality. But we do both our children and ourselves a great disservice when we avoid the topic of sex altogether or assign an almost mystical, forbidden aura to it. By placing it on the pedestal of That Which Shall Remain Unnamed, we allot shame and even negative importance to it in our children's minds.

I chose to approach talking about sex with Della from the framework with which I began this chapter. I told her that sex is a crucial element of God's good design for marriage between one man and one woman, that God had literally created woman from man, and that they were made to fit together, physically and emotionally, like two pieces of a puzzle. I used all the anatomically correct terms that so often make us squirm, but she just nodded and listened with wide, calm eyes.

After I had finished, I asked her if she had anything she wanted to ask and assured her that she is welcome to come to me with *any* concerns or questions that she has. I told her I knew that it could all be a little awkward but that I would rather she hear it from me than anyone else. Her response let me know that all the preparation we had been doing by giving her as much information from Scripture as she could handle at that time had paid off. "Why should I feel awkward about any of this?" she said. "God designed it, and it's a good thing, so what is there to be embarrassed about?"

I was so blessed by her emotional poise, but I can't say I was completely surprised—partly because I know my daughter well and partly because I knew this was not her first exposure to the concept. Rather, it was a culmination of years of gradually increasing knowledge. Again, I'm not saying that ours is the only way to go about this, but I am saying that taking it upon ourselves to be our children's first touchpoint for this sensitive topic is essential.

## The Ugly Truth About Porn

I do believe it is possible to take "openness" with our children on the topic of sex too far, though, especially when it comes to practices that are clearly wrong. Ali Wentworth (George Stephanopoulos's wife) has said that she would watch pornography with her teenage daughters. She explained her unconventional choice by reasoning that "You can't stop them. You certainly can't stop them. If they look at porn, I would look at the porn with them." She argues that she does this for the sake of education. An article about her approach on *She Knows* applauds this as a reasonable perspective and concludes that "it's the best way to prep [kids] to enjoy it in a healthy way (and maintain a healthy sex life of their own) when they're ready."[6]

The "it" the article references is presumably porn itself, which means that the author is starting from the assumption that there is a healthy way to consume images of others having sex. This supposition flies in the face of the growing mountain of evidence that pornography is far from harmless and is, in fact, the opposite of healthy. More and more studies link pornography with addiction, sexual dysfunction, abuse, sex trafficking, and exploitation.

To ignore any or all of these issues is dangerous, regardless of your religious views. And yet Wentworth's choice to expose her daughters to porn is not grounded in a desire to illustrate how utterly unredeemable it is. (There are far better ways to underscore how destructive it is, if that's your goal, than by viewing it.) Instead, she wants to show her girls that porn is not a realistic portrayal of women's bodies or sexual behavior. While I agree with that part, I do not track with anything else about her ideology. A simple explanation of pornography's lack of realism—rather than a show-and-tell session—*would* be sufficient if that were its only problem. But such an explanation fails to address the slimy underbelly of a multibillion-dollar industry that profits from addiction and exploitation.

It is our job to tell our children that porn is destructive to both men and women because it endangers marriages before they even begin. Because how could a "normal" woman hope to measure up to the airbrushed, spray-tanned, liposuctioned versions of "reality" that are just a click away? Porn-induced erectile dysfunction—the inability to be aroused by your real-life partner—is a real thing, and it is devastating to real people every day. Not only that, but there has been a marked increase in recent years in the number of girls who consume pornography, which means that this is not an exclusively male problem.

So why aren't more secular sources acknowledging these truths and calling pornography out for the evil cancer that it is? To some extent, I believe that our culture refuses to categorically denounce pornography because doing so would belie their claim that sex outside of marriage is no big deal. After all, if extramarital sex doesn't really matter, then why should watching someone else do it matter either? Of course, biblical Christians know that it matters because, as we discussed in the last chapter, what we consume with our eyes often worms its way deep into our minds and hearts.

## Ancient but Not Tired

To anyone who claims that it's naive to teach our children that God's design for physical intimacy is limited to one man and one woman within marriage, and that such teaching is nothing more than a tired old trope, our answer must be a hearty, "No!" God's stance on the sanctity of the marriage bed may be old (Garden of Eden old), but it is far from tired. Hebrews 13:4 (ESV) makes his views clear: "Let marriage be held in honor among all, and let the marriage bed be undefiled, for God will judge the sexually immoral and adulterous." And Jesus took it a step further in Matthew 5 when he said that merely looking at a woman lustfully is committing adultery of the heart. So even the excuse of watching pornography to "spice things up a bit" within a marriage will not fly. It is this radical approach to purity, both before and within marriage, that worldly culture cannot comprehend.

In the same article from *She Knows*, the author quotes a "Portland-based family educator" as saying, "There are good studies that show abstinence-only education does not work." I don't know what these "good" studies are, but I actually agree our kids need more than abstinence-only directives. If we simply beat the "don't have sex" drum, I can only imagine the percentage of kids who actually march to it will be incredibly low. After all, media makes sex look, well, *sexy*. They use it to sell everything from beer to cars to vacuums. So why *wouldn't* we want a piece of that?

We would. And we do. And that's natural.

God has placed a sexual drive within each of us, and that is good—*within* the parameters of his perfect design for marriage. However, if we fail to explain *why* that caveat is so important and instead merely insist on toeing the abstinence line, we will encounter significant resistance from kids who feel like we are robbing them of the fun that society (and their hormones) assures them they're due.

## Waiting for Marriage Is Sexy

And this is ultimately why a mediocre approach of passivity or caving to popular cultural narratives does such damage to our children's views of intimacy. We don't paint saving sex until marriage in the alluring light it deserves. "Purity culture," with its emphasis on pledges and special rings, begins with its heart in the right place, I believe. But, as with any other prescriptive approach, it can easily veer into legalism and fearmongering. I've heard from many readers who were frightened into abstinence by dire warnings about God's wrath, only to rebel later. Many others entered marriage with dismally low expectations after hearing about a "wife's duty to her husband" from older women who acted like sex was a (disagreeable) box to be checked.

Instead, we have the opportunity as mamas to show our children just how enjoyable and joyful giving affection to our husband (and only our husband) can be! When we emphasize God's good plan for sex in marriage and how fulfilling it is to exercise self-control in the short term for a long-term relationship free of sexual baggage, comparison, and past hurt, we give our kids hope for a healthy and, yes, pure marriage.

I know our society assumes that abstinence from sex when our teenage hormones are demanding the opposite is impossible, even outright unnatural. But neither my husband nor I have had any other sexual partners. Many others in our Christian circle who got married around the same time have the same story. And none of our relationships have suffered as a result. On the contrary, the trust and intimacy that comes from knowing that your sexual history is shared with no one else produces incredible peace and freedom to be yourself in the bedroom.

For my part, I didn't choose chastity begrudgingly because I was bullied into it by well-meaning but heavy-handed parents or church leaders. Yes, my parents taught me what the Bible has to say about sex before marriage, but I never felt threatened—merely encouraged that however appealing the world made premarital sex look, it would be all the more fulfilling and exciting if shared only with my future spouse. Not only that, but I saw for myself the results of sexually promiscuous behavior in my peers, and it never even remotely resembled the glamorous portrayal of it in movies like *Dirty Dancing* or *Pretty Woman* (two "feel-good" classics that teach all the wrong lessons about casual sex).

Shaun felt the same way, although his story is different since he held strong to his beliefs in saving physical intimacy for marriage while he was still an unbeliever. He even went so far as to roll up a comforter and place it in the middle of his bed as a barrier when his girlfriend at the time stayed over due to car trouble. When I asked him why he felt such a conviction to wait, he said this: "I did not want my future wife to have been with anybody else, and I assumed she would feel the same. If I'd had sex before marriage, I would have felt like I was

Abstinence for the sake of pure marriages is as sexy as it gets. Let's proclaim it boldly to our kids.

cheating on my future spouse." I believe that the Lord was gracious to gift my husband with a special insight into the beauty of an exclusive sexual relationship between a married man and woman. He didn't see sex as casual or blasé but as sacred and something to be cherished.

He's right. It is.

And if we as Christian mamas are concerned about portraying sex in a biblically accurate way (and we should be), then we must "woman up" and be willing to talk about God's good design so that our children are not bowled over by a worldly agenda that promotes and confirms ungodly choices, gender confusion, and above all, a misguided outlook that abstinence before marriage is only for uptight goody two-shoes or those who can't "get any."

We know the truth. Abstinence for the sake of pure marriages is as sexy as it gets. Let's proclaim it boldly to our kids.

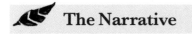 **The Narrative**

| MEDIOCRE MOTHERHOOD | CHRISTLIKE MOTHERHOOD |
| --- | --- |
| Leaves explanations about sex to "someone else" | Sees "sex ed" as a job for parents |
| Allows worldly values to dominate the narrative | Explains sex from a biblical perspective |
| Fails to understand the importance of preparing kids for godly intimacy | Knows what's at stake in a world full of sexual confusion and hurt |

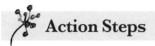

## Action Steps

- Memorize and meditate on Genesis 2:24 (ESV): "Therefore a man shall leave his father and his mother and hold fast to his wife, and they shall become one flesh."

- Develop a plan for talking about sex with your kids that conveys God's good plan for it.

- Take stock of technology, and assess whether your kids have access to sexual information they are not ready for.

## Questions

Do I have a biblical view of sex? If not, why?

Why, when God has so clearly given it his stamp of approval inside marriage, am I so nervous to talk to my kids about sex?

What are the benefits of my kids hearing about sex from me instead of from the world?

## Prayer

*Lord, you have given us the good gift of sex in marriage.
Thank you! Help us to clearly convey the joy that intimacy
with our spouse can bring and to do it boldly in a way
that combats the lies our culture seeks to spread.*

# You Don't Have to Do It All

## ACCEPTING HELP IS A GOOD IDEA

I get asked all the time whether I have "help." Our second DIY build is large, and there seems to be a general fascination with how I could possibly manage to keep it clean (news flash: It's almost never all clean at the same time) while homeschooling, blogging, teaching fitness classes, cooking dinner, and doing general life stuff. I feel the same way about many of my friends—online and in person—who have a number of spinning plates. I am in awe of their ability to do so much at once. But the truth is I don't know very many women who aren't fairly adept at cooking dinner while answering an email and bandaging a boo-boo. Multitasking seems to be in our blood.

But just because we are *capable* of doing many things at once does not mean that we don't get overwhelmed, feel inadequate, or sometimes allow a few of our spinning plates to fly across the room and smash into the wall.

## Doing It All Is a Myth

There is no one—I repeat, *no one*—who does it all. Just as we talked about back at the beginning of this book, no two good mamas look alike. With our different interests and personalities come different strengths and priorities. What remains constant, though, is that none of us is capable of nailing every category of everything all the time. There are simply too many categories. If we are in a season of ease, our capacity might expand to include five or six things we do really well. But there will always be that one area (at least) in which we could improve. I believe the Lord has designed us this way for two reasons:

1. If we were ever to reach the point of dominating in every facet of life at every moment, we would be hard-pressed to recognize our ever-present need of him. Our faith would be in our own abilities, rather than in the One from whom they flow.

2. If we were killing it all the time, we might never recognize our need for others.

No man is an island. And while I doubt many mothers have ever pictured themselves as an island—more like the hub of one of those many-armed, spinning kiddie rides at the carnival—we sometimes behave as if we should be able to do a superhuman number of tasks with zero help.

*Why would we think that when we are struggling and in need of help, accepting it is a shameful act that makes us "less than" in any way?*

At least a fourth of the twenty-four hours we each get in a day must be spent sleeping if we want our bodies and brains to continue functioning at even close to full capacity. So why would we ever assume that anyone else is capable of fitting more things into a day than is humanly possible? And why would we think that when we are struggling and in need of help, accepting it is a shameful act that makes us "less than" in any way?

These are questions I have grappled with personally for years, even long after we first made the decision to hire a neighbor to help with cleaning once Evy and

Nola were born. I can still recall the curious mixture of relief comingled with disappointment in myself. I was a homeschooling mama of five children, ages six and under, and I was not doing all the things. Or rather, I was doing lots and lots of things but not all of them well. My laundry often sat in a basket at the end of my bed (or sometimes in untidy piles on the floor) for two weeks at a time. Digging through the basket for clean undies was like a daily treasure hunt. And yet I still felt like a failure for hiring help (even though I clearly needed it).

## Prideful, Not Powerful

I experienced the same tension when we first hired my mom to help with homeschooling two days a week. Our girl twins were in their "change-clothes-seventeen-times-a-day" phase, and I was pregnant with our sixth. But by gum, a real woman should have been able to figure out how to keep the clothes in the drawers while fighting nausea and fatigue, scrubbing the toilets, teaching math, and getting a home-cooked meal on the table on time. Or so I told myself as I trailed my mom around, trying to instruct my kids in the same things she was already teaching them because just letting her do the job I was paying her to do would clearly indicate that I was a deadbeat.

I think it's pretty obvious that I was being ridiculous (and prideful). As counterintuitive as it may sound in a book about bucking mediocrity to admit to needing help, the truth is that insisting on doing everything yourself often produces lower quality results than being willing to acknowledge your limits and outsource when possible. Of course, there is a bit of a mixed message in our Western bootstrap culture: Either it takes a village, or we're supposed to be Supergirl in her Fortress of Solitude. Neither extreme is scripturally sound. The Bible never exhorts us to recruit every friend, neighbor, godmother, and postman to tackle the essential challenge of teaching our children well. Getting that many people to align meaningfully with our core values as a Christian family would be nearly impossible. But neither does the Bible say that we should shun all offers of help. Hebrews 10:24-25 says, "Let us consider how we may spur one another on toward love and good deeds, not giving up meeting together, as some are in the habit of doing, but encouraging one another."

There is a bit of a mixed message in our Western bootstrap culture: Either it takes a village, or we're supposed to be Supergirl in her Fortress of Solitude.

Community and the practical support that it offers is important to our Christian walk. To some extent, all our answers to "Do you have help?" should be yes—in an ideal world. Because hopefully we have the support of our Christian family at least. We should also be providing help to others in whatever capacity we can. It's a continual ebb and flow of blessing and being blessed.

## Christians Need Each Other

The manuscript for this book was due right after Christmas, and I will never forget the weeks that led up to it (Christmas and my deadline). We had Titus's and Tobias's lip and tongue ties revised, which messed with the strides we'd made in sleeping longer stretches at night. The poor little guys were miserable for a solid week. And I was equally woebegone from lack of sleep and nursing soreness. The day after their revision, I rear-ended a truck and trailer in our brand-new fifteen-passenger van. The trailer didn't sustain a scratch, but our van was undrivable. Later that week, I developed an ulcer so gnarly that the entire left side of my head throbbed nonstop for days. That Sunday, I took my youngest seven to church alone because my husband and oldest kids were out of town, and Evy and Nola had been invited for a playdate after church with a sweet family. They had been so helpful with their older brothers and sister gone, and I was determined to get them there.

But nothing went right that morning. I wrenched my back getting out of bed (this is late thirties with ten kids) and couldn't bend over to lift my thirty-two-pound toddler. So of course, the only thing he wanted was to be held, and he expressed his disappointment that I could not comply with great, ahem, *enthusiasm*, complete with full, facedown body slams onto the bathroom tile. It took a while, but I finally got everybody dressed in their Sunday best and loaded in the car. But, as I was pulling out of our garage and paying less attention to the garage doors than to Honor's meltdown over his car seat buckle, I crunched the side mirror of our old van that we had borrowed back from the friends who bought it. I then spent ten minutes hobbling stiffly through the house looking for duct tape, finally locating some in a pink floral design. Oh, and did I mention it was pouring rain?

SPUR
ONE ANOTHER ON
TOWARD LOVE AND
GOOD DEEDS.
HEBREWS 10:24

By the time we all lurched into the church foyer, dripping and too late to find a seat among the Christmas crowds, my mouth was set in a grim line of resignation to my fate—that is, until a fellow mom approached and asked, "How are you, friend?" And my eyes brimmed with the tears I'd been keeping at bay for at least an hour. Her words as she hugged me were like "apples of gold in settings of silver" (Proverbs 25:11): "There is grace and mercy for this too."

The Lord illustrated just how true that was as my friend ushered me to overflow seating in the fellowship hall and set my kids up with coloring sheets and snacks. And again when the same family who had invited Evy and Nola extended the invitation for me and my little boys as well, so I could have a place to nurse my babies and wouldn't have to worry about rustling up food for the others. And yet again when the husband of a friend insisted on running through the rain to drive "my" van (which now sported a super stylish floral duct tape bandage on its side mirror) under the covered pavilion while we waited.

Those people were Jesus to me on a day when I needed them.

It was my turn a few days later when a friend from church posted a comment on my social media about having a bad week and a bare pantry. I had been having a bit of a pity party that I wasn't in a place of being able to bless others, that my deadlines and fussy babies were preventing me from spreading Christmas cheer. And the Lord nudged me and said, "Her pantry is bare. You can do something about that."

So I got on my phone and placed a pickup order for groceries for my friend. And wouldn't you know it? My doldrums disappeared!

*That is the beauty of blessing others. We do it for them, but we benefit greatly in return. I need to remember this when I am tempted to clutch my problems tightly to my chest so no one can see and offer a helping hand.*

Because that is the beauty of blessing others. We do it for them, but we benefit greatly in return. I need to remember this when I am tempted to clutch my problems tightly to my chest so no one can see and offer a helping hand. In doing so, I am robbing them of an opportunity to give and receive the blessing of help.

## You Have More Help Than You Think

Now, maybe you're reading this and thinking, "That's all well and good, Abbie. But I haven't found a church home yet, and I live nowhere near family. All my kids are little. Also, there's no way that we could afford to hire help."

I get it. When we "only" had two under two, we were in much the same boat. But if you're reading this book, you almost certainly have a wonderful source of help sitting nearby, possibly twiddling your hair or tugging on your elbow for a snack. Because learning to be helpful starts at a young age. Or at least it should.

Secular mom culture—what I have titled the culture of mediocre motherhood—disagrees. The same people whose feathers are ruffled at the concept of "training" kids get just as bent out of shape about requiring them to help. Modern society has adopted a viewpoint foreign to past generations: the notion that childhood requires complete freedom from responsibility for the simple (if misguided) reason that small humans are incapable of shouldering any.

It's a conclusion that does a great disservice to our kids and to those whom they encounter. My dear friend, who is an amazing mama of twelve—and whose children are some of the kindest, most thoughtful, and most enjoyable I have ever met—has even been accused of having more children simply so she can have "slave labor." Of course, the irony of such a jab is that these are the same people who claim that kids are hopeless slobs. They're at least a little bit right. Kids are not hopeless, but any thinking person knows that the more children we have, the more messes we have as well. Having more in no way increases our chances of a tidy home.

Unless, of course, we are willing to put in the work to teach them to be helpful.

Too often, our frustrations in this area stem from a paradoxical form of laziness that I have been tempted to adopt at times. It goes a little something like this: "Cleaning with kids is torture. I could do this so much faster myself. I'll just plop them in front of some cartoons and get this sorted." There are times, especially with tiny children, when this is the only way the living room will get picked up before our in-laws walk in the door, and that's fine. But when it becomes our crutch, we have a problem.

Biblically excellent motherhood acknowledges that while allowing my children to play and be little is important, shirking my responsibility to teach them skills and attitudes that will serve them and others well as they grow is wrong. Yep, I said it.

Training up the next generation of helpers may, in the beginning stage, feel like getting a root canal while gargling rubbing alcohol, but the benefits—to them! to you! to others!—are manifold. Not only that, but having children who are accustomed to open doors for others, clear tables after dinner, and ask the all-important question, "May I help you with something?" will present opportunities to share the gospel. When our children bless members of our community with their thoughtfulness, and those people comment or ask questions, we can always give the glory to God. "We love because he first loved us" (1 John 4:19), remember?

Of course, in practical terms, when we pour ourselves into teaching and training our children, we reap the benefits as well.

## "Many Hands" and All That

Years ago, when my oldest was only about ten, I found myself falling into bed each night in a state of complete exhaustion and discouragement. My mom was still coming twice a week for school, but we had long since stopped hiring our neighbor to help with cleaning. The kids and I were doing a decent job of getting to things during the day, but by the end of it, after homeschooling and discipling, diaper changing and dinner prepping, I was spent. And yet the dishes were still waiting in the sink, and the crumbs had not magically swept themselves into the trash.

Shaun and the kids were oblivious to my distress because we would often watch a show together during the evenings, and while I could see the television from the kitchen, their backs were turned to me as I scrubbed pans and swept floors. Finally, one night, I told my husband how much I was struggling to keep going by the end of the day. And just like he did with the Penny Reward System, he responded with practical wisdom.

He proposed that we establish a period of nightly family cleanup. We would distribute the tasks in an age-appropriate way, and then we would set timers and get to work. And so our "evening routine" was born. I had already set a similar system in place for the morning, but it had somehow never occurred to me that "many hands make light work" would be even more applicable at the end of the day when I needed help the most. Maybe it was because I didn't want my kids to have to do "too much" or because I was, yet again, adhering to an unrealistic idea of what I "should" be able to accomplish by myself.

Whatever the hang-up, our nightly routine lifted a huge burden from my shoulders. What had been an hour-long slog at the end of a full day became a half-hour session of communal cleaning. Not only did we accomplish more with more helping hands, but we had way more fun—blasting music, singing, and dancing as we worked. And in the process, we conveyed several things to our children:

1. If you contribute to the mess, you contribute to the cleanup.

2. You are capable of learning new skills and doing them with excellence. (When my oldest two learned to fold washcloths, they cried. Literally. When Evy and Nola first started unloading the dishwasher at age five, they were convinced it was too big a job. When Theo learned to put away clothes in his room, he thought he might die from the weight of such hard work. Spoiler: They're all still alive, and none of them thinks his or her job is a big deal anymore.)

3. Your contributions are valuable and important to our family.

4. Helping is fun.

# Blessed to Be a Blessing

Teaching our kids to be helpful holds the same truths as it does for adults. They are blessed to be a blessing, and although most of the opportunities for this will start in their own home, the mentality will overflow into others' lives as well. The children of the family who had us over for lunch after my "terrible, horrible, no good, very bad" morning were as much a blessing as their parents—entertaining my littles, cleaning up their messes, and helping me carry babies to the car when I left. They clearly were being taught the right lessons about helping in their home.

So circling back around to the question that I get asked all the time—"Do you have help?"—yes, I do. I have my mom, my husband, my kids, my friends at church, and my neighbor's daughter whom I hired to babysit my youngest three a few hours a week while I finished this book. By the time you read this, we may have hired someone to help with cleaning again. It's an ongoing discussion, especially during weeks when our morning and evening cleanup routines are disrupted, and the toilets are looking grimy.

There is no shame in receiving help. And there is great joy in extending it. It wasn't good for Adam to do his work alone. And it's not good for us either. So the next time someone offers to help, respond with a resounding, "Yes! Thank you!" And then offer to help the next person you see in need. You will be amazed at the difference it makes in your life and theirs.

 **The Narrative**

| MEDIOCRE MOTHERHOOD | CHRISTLIKE MOTHERHOOD |
|---|---|
| Is too prideful to accept help | Is humble enough to admit weakness |
| Wallows in defeat and overwhelm | Rejoices in the give-and-take of being helpful |
| Views kids as obstacles to productivity | Considers kids as valuable assets |

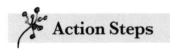 **Action Steps**

- Memorize and meditate on Galatians 6:2 (ESV): "Bear one another's burdens, and so fulfill the law of Christ."
- Write out a list of areas in which you need help and areas in which you could offer it.
- Make a plan to encourage and allow your kids to help at home in meaningful ways, even if it's inconvenient at first.

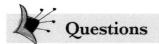 **Questions**

Why do I sometimes feel guilty for requesting or accepting help?

What are practical ways I can "bear another's burden" this week?

How can I convey value and dignity to my children by letting them bless me with help?

 **Prayer**

*Lord, you promise never to leave us or forsake us (Hebrews 13:5), and yet we often act as if we must do everything on our own. Teach us to see the deep joy in both offering help and allowing others to help us.*

# Emotions Are Not Facts

## WHY SURROUNDING OURSELVES WITH TRUTH-SPEAKERS IS ESSENTIAL TO BIBLICAL MOTHERHOOD

I knew I wanted to end this book with a chapter about the importance of not momming alone. I offered to be your boot camp instructor, your cheerleader, and your pal in the introduction, and I hope I've been able to deliver at least a little.

But you and I will probably never meet this side of heaven. And just like we talked about in the last chapter, community is vital to keeping us going when we are struggling and in need of help. Community is also crucial when we might be doing just fine physically, but we find ourselves emotionally going off the rails, or we see a friend doing the same.

## Circumstances Do Not Determine Truth

Emotions, for women especially, are some of the most simultaneously beneficial and harmful things in the world. Emotions help us make it through long nights of feeding babies (because we feel happy when we cuddle their squishy bodies). Emotions also make us want to figuratively throw in the towel when we discover that someone yet again literally threw towels all over the bathroom floor and didn't bother to pick them up (because we feel personally offended by our family's inability to value a clean house as much as we do).

And above all, emotions ride upon the carriage of circumstance and depend heavily on how many bumps in the road it strikes. When life is easy, our emotions say, "Ah, yes. This is how it is meant to be. This is right and good." But when life is hard, they sputter, "Hey, wait. I didn't sign up for this. This is wrong and bad."

I'd love to say that I'm oversimplifying things. Except I'm not. The day before I wrote these words, I was feeling hurt by something my husband had *not* said. (Yes, you read that correctly.) I spent a good chunk of my day trying to distract myself from my own emotions. We climbed in his truck to go on a date, but I could not seem to get myself in a date-night mood. Because he still hadn't responded to the emotional elephant in the room. My circumstances would not "allow" my emotions to relax. And then he did say the very thing that I had been waiting for, and instantly, the cloud of tension and confusion and, yes, anger lifted from my soul.

Here's the thing: I'm not a terribly emotional person. It was only because it was my husband involved, and it was something deeply important to me, that it held such sway. And yet the fact remains that until my circumstances were "rectified," I did not feel better.

## The Shifting Sands of Feelings

Now, we are not robots. So the reality that our feelings and our circumstances are intricately intertwined should surprise no one. We've already established the fact that Jesus was sad in response to sad circumstances. Everyone knows the shortest verse in the Bible is "Jesus wept," and his tears were not happy ones.

Difficulties emerge when instead of acknowledging that some emotions are legitimate and warranted while others are fueled by hormones, lack of sleep, or a recent viewing of *Steel Magnolias*, we insist that our feelings are our "truth."

"I feel, therefore I am" is a tricky declaration at best. After all, if we feel angry, does that then define us? The same question applies to fear, jealousy, sadness, or even happiness. What happens when our feelings suddenly shift?

And yet terrifyingly, in modern culture, I see feelings touted as the primary determinant of what we believe, how we choose our careers, the number of kids we have, how we school them, whether we stay faithful to our marriages, which gender we "identify as," and on and on.

The motto "If it feels good, do it" has been around for ages. But lately, "If it feels bad, don't do it" might be leading the charge as the subconscious catchphrase of the day. This is a sobering consideration when so much of motherhood consists of doing things because they are right, even when they "feel bad" (pushing babies out of our bodies, getting up at night to feed them, making nutritious food when we're tired, giving the hug when we're "touched out," to name a few). The payoff is well worth the pain, but how will we ever find that out for ourselves if we're so busy avoiding emotional and physical discomfort that we never try?

The culture of mediocre motherhood says, "All feelings are valid." This means if we wake up in a funk, we're not required to "adult." (The fact that this particular word has become a verb says a lot about our society.) Our children will only get whatever we have left to give at any moment of the day, and that's okay.

But it's really not.

Our kids deserve to know that even when Mama is struggling, even when she feels tired or overwhelmed, she will make an effort for their sake. Y'all, hear me: I am not saying that "an effort" on the days when we are not our best and brightest needs to look like homemade cake and handicrafts. I'm actually not saying that any days need to look like that. For our family, struggle-bus days look like reading books aloud, spending time outside, watching a nature show together on the couch, and eating rotisserie chicken and fruit for dinner. Knowing our limits is healthy. Whipping around like a kite caught in an emotional thunderstorm is not—especially if our children are the ones holding the strings.

Knowing our limits is healthy. Whipping around like a kite caught in an emotional thunderstorm is not— especially if our children are the ones holding the strings.

# Giving Thanks in All Circumstances
## (Even on the Internet)

I wrote every bit of this book in the year of our Lord 2020, the year that will forever be imprinted on our collective memory as one of the worst in recent history. And it will be remembered so distinctly as such because of the phenomenon of social media. Nothing cemented the fate of 2020 as a year of fear and loathing more than the ability of everyone in the entire world to get on the internet and grumble about it.

And no particular social media gripe session exemplified the problem of letting our emotions run amok quite so thoroughly for me as one that I stumbled upon about making dinner. This poster was done with dinner. If dinner were a person, she would punch him in the nose. Thanks to quarantine, she'd been making dinner for something like fifteen straight nights, and she was over it. Completely. Let her family eat whatever they could forage. She was having "wine dinner."

The post itself was written with an exquisite blend of exasperation and farce. It was a funny post. Or at least it would have been were it not for the thousands of women who commented about feeling utterly defeated at having to make dinner for their families every night. It seemed that many viewed it as a genuine hardship. But more than anything, I believe that to most, the constant task of coming up with something for dinner when they were used to eating out or ordering in was a metaphor for how upended their lives felt as a result of COVID-19 and its lockdowns.

They couldn't go to work. Their children were constantly around, asking for snacks, needing help with their distance learning homework, making demands. They'd been stripped of their "me" time and their community. And so they turned to the internet for comfort and commiseration.

And woe betide anyone who had the audacity to even mildly hint to this disgruntled group of self-proclaimed Christians that making dinner for our families might possibly qualify as an act of worship, per Romans 12:1.

In contrast, I did not see this response from genuinely biblical Christian posts on social media. There was the acknowledgment that our current circumstances were not ideal. But there was also a call to look for the good, to focus outside of ourselves on those who were enduring legitimate distress, and yes, to give thanks in all circumstances (1 Thessalonians 5:18).

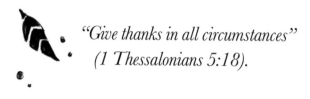

*"Give thanks in all circumstances"*
*(1 Thessalonians 5:18).*

What a truly radical approach—so radical, in fact, that I often saw people who made reasonable attempts to encourage others to stay focused on Christ attacked as "insensitive." Rather than be reminded of all the good things that have often come from suffering (yes, even the suffering of nightly dinner prep), many women wanted to stay deep in their feelings, wallowing luxuriously in the "no-shame zone" that the "wine dinner" poster declared her corner of the internet to be.

*The Bible makes it clear we are to cling to Jesus in our devastation. And it is difficult to do that when we are being given constant permission to despair and complain by our peers and those we "follow" in the social media world.*

Don't misunderstand me: 2020 was hard. For some, it was devastating. But the Bible makes it clear we are to cling to Jesus in our devastation. And it is difficult to do that when we are being given constant permission to despair and complain by our peers and those we "follow" in the social media world.

## Whom We Follow Matters

And this is why it is so very important—life-changing, actually—to choose our friends and influences wisely.

My best friend, Lindsay, is a constant source of encouragement and life to me. She's the artist who created all the delightful artwork throughout this book, and she's one half of our art print collaboration, Paint and Prose. She is exactly the sharpening influence that Proverbs 27:17 talks about. We have walked the trails near our gym for untold hours through the years, with various combinations of babies in strollers or strapped to our chests, and conversations with her always hone my convictions and focus my priorities. I come away from her presence refreshed, recharged, and redoubled in my desire to pursue Jesus. I can say this, to varying degrees, about at least a dozen other women in my life right now. But as I mentioned before, this has not always been the case. I prayed long and hard for friendships full of truth, conviction, and hope. And I prayed to be allowed to bring those qualities to others as well.

The Lord answered my prayers, for which I am so grateful. But I still have to continually examine the voices that I allow to speak into my life, along with the postures that I assume online and at home, to determine whether I am aligned with the world or with Christ.

As 1 John 4:1 (ESV) says, "Beloved, do not believe every spirit, but test the spirits to see whether they are from God, for many false prophets have gone out into the world."

*We, as Christian mamas, forsake whatever tugs our hearts toward the mediocrity of loving ease and comfort over the excellence of taking up our crosses to follow Jesus.*

This means that we, as Christian mamas, forsake whatever tugs our hearts toward the mediocrity of loving ease and comfort over the excellence of taking up our crosses to follow Jesus. Some friendships, books, and accounts—even those that claim to be Christian—may not survive this testing. Certainly, any advice that prods us toward an attitude of entitlement or self-indulgence is suspect. When godly conviction and a desire to focus on the good the Lord is doing are called "shaming" and shunted aside in favor of collective self-pity, take notice. It may feel good to vent at first, but soon we will find ourselves mired in discontentment and resentment if we fix our eyes on anything but Jesus, the Author and Finisher of our faith.

An online friend once posted these words in reference to the seemingly endless days of mothering little ones, and her post perfectly summed up the struggle that many young moms have: "I realized I'd been reading the wrong books and envying the wrong Instagram accounts. My misery loved company, and I was seeking it more than I sought the Lord."

It would behoove all of us to adopt this self-aware attitude, but there will inevitably be those who cling to their "right to be wrecked" by motherhood and never arrive at a conviction to give thanks in all circumstances. The Bible has exciting news for anyone who has ears to hear it, though. Friends, if we are in Christ, we are a new creation! The old has gone, the new is here! (2 Corinthians 5:17). We don't have to be enslaved to our culture's assumption that "surviving" our kids means a daily diet of wine and Starbucks or that Netflix and Target runs are the only coping mechanisms available to the modern mom. (As someone who doesn't drink wine or coffee, doesn't have Netflix, and doesn't shop at Target, I am grateful that Jesus is better, or I would be sunk.)

## Scripture > Every Other Influence

Neither do we have to bow to the tyranny of our emotions. Regardless of our circumstances, we can choose biblically excellent motherhood with Christ by our side and—Lord willing—other godly women in stride with us. If I could guarantee that you would glean any wisdom from this book, it would be that God's Word is able to change lives. It is alive and powerful, sharper than any

_Therefore,_
_if anyone is in Christ,_
_he is a new Creation._

2 CORINTHIANS 5:17 ESV

double-edged sword and able to pierce so deeply as to divide soul and spirit. It can even discern the thoughts and intents of the heart. But that wisdom is readily available in Hebrews 4:12, so why do you need me? Maybe for this: to remind you that no other source of knowledge, understanding, or comfort will last longer, effect more practical change, or provide true hope like Scripture. Without it, we are truly sunk.

But we cannot partake of its benefits if we do not read it. We cannot preach the Truth that tames our unruly emotions if we do not memorize it. And we cannot encourage each other to look for God's goodness if we have not first meditated on it in his Word.

It's awfully hard to stage a revolution with one person. I'm proposing that we form a sisterhood of Bible-believing, truth-speaking mamas who refuse to conform to the worldly status quo. Who boldly declare that motherhood is a calling, not a concession. Who rebel against the culture of mediocre motherhood because Christ-centered motherhood is radicalism in its most sanctifying, soul-impacting form.

I'm not much of a rebel usually. But I'll gladly lead a revolt against a view of motherhood that strips women of hope and paints children as a burden. It is for freedom that Christ has set us free. His work on the cross has won the war. But it's still a daily battle to see motherhood—and our kids—with the eyes of Jesus. I know for a fact the effort is worth it, and I'd love for you to join me in the fight.

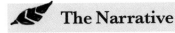
## The Narrative

| MEDIOCRE MOTHERHOOD | CHRISTLIKE MOTHERHOOD |
|---|---|
| Makes life decisions based on emotion | Bases life decisions on God's Word |
| Believes all emotions are valid | Knows that feelings can be deceiving |
| Resents the encouragement to rejoice in all things | Welcomes the opportunity to give thanks in all circumstances |
| Surrounds herself with an echo chamber of complaint | Chooses godly women for accountability |

## Action Steps

- Memorize and meditate on Jeremiah 17:9 (ESV): "The heart is deceitful above all things, and desperately sick; who can understand it?"

- Assess the influences you allow to have a voice in your life. Are they speaking gospel truth or the empty "gospel" of feelings?

- Commit to gauging your emotions against the guide of Scripture. Journaling is a great way to do this!

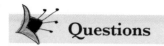

## Questions

How do I allow my circumstances to dictate my emotions?

Who should I be turning to for truth and encouragement in Christ?

Why are platitudes about "following your heart" ultimately empty?

## Prayer

*Lord, we know that you experienced the full range of human emotions in your time on this earth. And yet you did not sin. Help us to follow your example as we bring our emotions under the Lordship of Jesus Christ and surround ourselves with godly sisters who will do the same.*

# Favorite Resources

This is a list of media our family enjoys and from which we have gleaned value.
It's hardly exhaustive, but we hope you'll find it helpful!

## Television Shows

*American Ninja Warrior*
*Anne of Green Gables*[a]
*Five Mile Creek*
*The Great British Baking Show*[b]
*Hornblower*[c]
*How It's Made*
*Little House on the Prairie*
*MythBusters Junior*
*Pride and Prejudice*[d]
*Shaun the Sheep*
*Tiny World*
*Wild Kratts*[e]
*Winnie the Pooh*[f]

## Movies

*Babe*
*Bolt*
*A Bug's Life*
*Chicken Run*
*The Chronicles of Narnia* series
*The Emperor's New Groove*
*The Lord of the Rings* series[g]
*My Fair Lady*
*The Hobbit*[h]
*Paddington* (1 and 2)
*The Princess Bride*
*Singin' in the Rain*
*Swiss Family Robinson*

---

a  The 1985 miniseries.

b  Some opportunities for discussion of ungodly lifestyles, but enjoyable for all ages.

c  Age twelve and older.

d  The 1995 miniseries from BBC.

e  Evolutionary perspective but informative and fun.

f  Even my older kids will sit and down and get sucked into this one.

g  Ages ten and older.

h  Ages ten and older.

# Books for Kids

All of Jane Austen's novels
100 Cupboards Trilogy by N.D. Wilson
Anne of Green Gables series by L.M. Montgomery
*Charlotte's Web* by E.B. White
Christian Heroes: Then and Now series by Janet and Geoff Benge[a]
The Chronicles of Narnia series by C.S. Lewis
Frog and Toad series by Arnold Lobel
The Green Ember series by S.D. Smith
*The Hobbit* by J.R.R. Tolkien
*Adventures of Huckleberry Finn* by Mark Twain
Little Britches series by Ralph Moody[b]
Little House on the Prairie series by Laura Ingalls Wilder
*Little Women* by Louisa May Alcott
The Lord of the Rings trilogy by J.R.R. Tolkien
The Penderwicks series by Jeanne Birdsall
Ramona series by Beverly Cleary
Tales of the Kingdom Trilogy by David and Karen Mains
The Wingfeather Saga by Andrew Peterson

# Books for Moms

*GraceLaced* by Ruth Chou Simons
*Grumpy Mom Takes a Holiday* by Valerie Woerner
*Honey for a Child's Heart* by Gladys Hunt
*Let Me Be a Woman* by Elisabeth Elliot
*Mama Bear Apologetics* by Hillary Morgan Ferrer
*The Read-Aloud Family* by Sarah Mackenzie
*Risen Motherhood* by Emily Jensen and Laura Wifler

---

a   An excellent source of Christian missionary biographies.

b   Contains some profanity.

# Acknowledgments

I can't stop typing until I've bragged on a few people, without whom this book either wouldn't exist in its finished form or would be considerably less enjoyable.

Jennifer, thank you for proofreading every single line of every single chapter and putting up with a self-proclaimed grammar lover's complete inability to remember how to hyphenate ages or use colons correctly. Your suggestions, insights, and yes, hyphen expertise were invaluable assets. As is your friendship.

Lindsay, I knew I wanted you to illustrate this book the moment it became a reality. Being your friend and business partner has been one of the greatest privileges of my entire life. Your talent astounds me. And your heart even more so.

Mama, you are the main reason this book exists in the first place. Your unfailing example of patience, servant-heartedness, practical wisdom, no-nonsense gumption, and reliance on the Lord has taught me more than I can express. You are truly the best.

Ezra, Simon, Della, Evy, Nola, Theo, Honor, Shiloh, Titus, and Tobias, I thank God every day that he entrusted you to me to love and teach and safeguard for his kingdom. Being your mama is my favorite, and I will never get tired of it. I love you.

Shaun (a.k.a. Alby), you are the best cheerleader, advice-giver, sentence-tweaker, father, provider, and husband a homeschooling mama-turned-author could ever dream up. Plus, you're hot. Which may seem irrelevant but totally isn't.

# Notes

1. Brené Brown, "In You Must Go: Harnessing the Force by Owning Our Stories," *Brené Brown* (blog), May 4, 2018.

2. Oswald Chambers, *My Utmost for His Highest: Updated Edition* (Grand Rapids, MI: Discovery House, 1992), entry for November 15, "What Is That to You?"

3. "Devotional: Into His Life's Work at Last," *GeorgeMuller.org*, August 9, 2018.

4. Sarah MacKenzie, "RAR #132: Books for Teens, and Why YA Is a Genre (Not a Reading Level)," *Read Aloud Revival* (podcast), July 8, 2019.

5. Brian Scudamore, "The Truth About Smartphone Addiction, and How to Beat It," *Forbes*, October 30, 2018.

6. Amelia Edelman, "Why Ali Wentworth Watches Porn with Her Kids," *She Knows*, July 10, 2020.

# About the Author

Hi there! I'm Abbie with an "ie," which is not nearly as iconic as "Anne with an e" but still makes me feel an affinity for one of my favorite literary chatterboxes.

Speaking of chatting + literature, I'm a homeschool-graduate-turned-high-school-language/English/ESL teacher who double majored in English and Spanish, so talking and good books are kind of my jam.

These days, you'll find me homeschooling my crew of ten rad kids, who range in age from 18 months to almost 16 years old (at the time this book is first published). We have two sets of identical twins—one set of girls, one set of boys—*and* (fun fact) they were born on the exact same day eight years apart! For a girl who never planned to have a double handful of kids and who specifically asked God to give her any kids he had in mind one at a time (ha!), you might think this daily reality of bottom-wiping, attitude-correcting, haircut-giving, Algebra-grading, errand-running, and dinner-prepping is a stretch.

And it certainly does stretch me in the best possible ways. But I can also look back and see that God was preparing me for "just such a time as this" long before we ever had our firstborn a whopping nine days before our first anniversary, and his grace is the thread that continues to weave our family together each day.

When I'm not busy being Mama, I'm teaching fitness classes, blogging at www.misformama.net (and @m.is.for.mama on social media), hosting guests in our home, or wallpapering something (it's becoming a problem). My husband, Shaun, and I have designed and built two DIY homes from scratch, both of which caused way less marital strife than most people would think (we *like* working together!).

I'm also an avid proponent of the inerrancy of Scripture and love to encourage women to test every trend of culture against the truth that is Jesus and his holy Word, the Bible.

I wish we could have a cup of ho-cho (hot chocolate) together (no coffee for me, thanks). But since we can't, I hope you'll be encouraged in the Lord by the things he has taught me and that I've shared with you in this book.

Welcome to the sisterhood of biblically excellent motherhood (by God's grace).